A Pocket Guide to Mentoring Higher Education Faculty

Also by Tammy Stone

Leading from the Middle: A Case-Study Approach to Academic Leadership for Associate and Assistant Deans

A Pocket Guide to Mentoring Higher Education Faculty

Making the Time, Finding the Resources

Tammy Stone

ROWMAN & LITTLEFIELD
Lanham • Boulder • New York • London

Published by Rowman & Littlefield
An imprint of The Rowman & Littlefield Publishing Group, Inc.
4501 Forbes Boulevard, Suite 200, Lanham, Maryland 20706
www.rowman.com

Unit A, Whitacre Mews, 26-34 Stannary Street, London SE11 4AB

British Library Cataloguing in Publication Information Available

Library of Congress Cataloging-in-Publication Data

Names: Stone, Tammy, 1961- author.
Title: A pocket guide to mentoring higher education faculty : making the time, finding the resources / Tammy Stone.
Description: Lanham, Maryland : Rowman & Littlefield, [2018] | Includes bibliographical references and index.
Identifiers: LCCN 2018011008 (print) | LCCN 2018021368 (ebook) | ISBN 9781475840933 (electronic) | ISBN 9781475840919 (cloth : alk. paper) | ISBN 9781475840926 (pbk. : alk. paper)
Subjects: LCSH: Mentoring in education—United States. | College teachers—In-service training—United States. | Universities and colleges—United States—Faculty.
Classification: LCC LB2331.72 (ebook) | LCC LB2331.72 .S76 2018 (print) | DDC 371.102—dc23
LC record available at https://lccn.loc.gov/2018011008

Printed in the United States of America

To all the senior faculty members that were willing to talk to me when I was just starting out and to any faculty members I may have helped since that time.
Pay it forward.

Contents

Preface

In an ideal world, a mentoring culture would exist at all universities. Mentoring cultures are those in which everyone in the university willingly mentors others and everyone (faculty and staff) has no hesitancy to ask for mentoring when they feel they need it. But in the real world, mentoring cultures are either restricted to a relatively small group (new or junior faculty) or difficult to identify. Further, asking for mentoring is seen as a sign of weakness for some.

Developing a mentoring culture is further hampered by the very nature of higher education, where individual scholars strive within their disciplines to make contributions to their field and their students. This system rewards us for being single-minded, solitary scholars who rarely stray from our own discipline and frequently subspecialty within our discipline.

Although you would be hard pressed to argue against the idea that we should strive for a mentoring culture at all levels and for all groups at a university, it takes work to obtain it. Part of this work is making a conscious effort to look beyond our own area of expertise and learn what the faculty and staff members around us do in their daily work lives. It requires we listen to discover what other people's goals and aspirations are for the future and accept that they may be different from our own. Second, we need to learn how to mentor in new and innovative ways; one size cannot possibly fit all for such a diverse group.

The classic model of mentoring involving a wise sage guiding a young colleague through the difficulties of a research agenda or career path still exists. It is not, however, the *only* model, and increasingly it is not the most common model. Mentoring, in fact, comes in many forms. It can be formal or informal; it can include the traditional mentor-mentee relationship but can also involve peer mentoring, mentoring up, and group mentoring.

There is a considerable body of literature on different mentoring models in monographs and journals such as the *Journal of Faculty Development* and the *International Journal of University Teaching and Faculty*. These are joined by more generalized journals on higher education that contain articles on mentoring, including the *Chronicle of Higher Education, Research in Higher Education, Higher Education Quarterly, Innovative Higher Education*, and *Educational Leadership*, to name only a few.

These journals contain scholarly works (both empirically based and using a focus-group format) from individuals trained specifically in and researching institutional research and higher education administration. These are individuals who run large mentoring programs, often at top-tiered schools. However, according to the Carnegie Classification of Institutions of Higher Education (n.d.), less than 10 percent fall into the category of PhD-granting, highly intensive research institutions. The remaining 90+ percent fall into other categories. Their faculties, staffs, and students are just as bright and work just as hard as their colleagues at the top-tiered institutions but live with a different set of constraints and a different work structure.

Divisions in institutions of higher education are often broken into several levels with different names. The Carnegie classification includes doctorate-granting, master-granting, bachelor-granting, and associate-granting intuitions, with several subdivisions in each of these categories. Others concentrate on state-run universities and colleges, making distinctions between flagship and branch campuses within a larger system.

Finally, Burton Clark (1987) suggests a better way to categorize colleges and universities is by their missions. Although he includes two-year institutions, I will leave these aside for the moment, because of the difference in the characterization of faculty workload. For schools that define faculty workload with three constituent parts (research, teaching, and service), he divides based on the relative importance placed on each. Specifically, he divides colleges and universities into research institutions (where research is emphasized over teaching for the tenure/tenure-track faculty), comprehensive institutions (where teaching and research are equally emphasized), and liberal arts colleges (where teaching is emphasized over research).

All of these categorization schemes have value, but none is perfect. As used here, top-tiered universities are institutions where large numbers of departments grant terminal degrees (PhD, JD, MD, MFA, DEd, etc.) and research dominates over teaching and service. These institutions have departments that are large with considerable depth of expertise not only in a broad disciplinary topic but also in subdisciplinary specialties.

Top-tiered schools are often seen as the flagship institution of a region and have long histories, large alumni bases, and considerable endowments. Many of these colleges and universities have large centers for faculty development that concentrate on all areas of faculty work that are staffed by individuals specifically trained in higher education administration and institutional research.

This can be contrasted with what are sometimes referred to as second-tier institutions. The second tier is a big and diverse category but includes institutions where research is important but does not dominate over teaching, where most departments lack PhD programs, and some or even many lack master's programs. Departments are often small so that there is a single representative of each branch of a discipline or, lacking sufficient personnel, faculty members cover several areas, including those in which they were not formally trained. The result is departments that have teaching breadth but not research depth in most areas of study and folks covering areas other than their specialties in the curriculum and student mentoring (this is the baccalaureate and master's programs of the Carnegie designation and the comprehensive and liberal arts colleges of Clark 1987).

Many of these schools either are small or were formed originally as branch campuses of larger educational systems so that their alumni base is smaller and their endowments are either small or nonexistent. Many of these schools either lack centers for faculty development or have centers that concentrate on teaching effectiveness only. That means the faculty at the department and division/school level must take on the role of mentoring, even though they were not formally trained in this task and they frequently need a mentor themselves. Little is actually written on mentoring specifically for these types of schools, particularly smaller schools in that classification, where everyone covers multiple areas and budgets are extremely limited, despite their ubiquity.

Having spent my academic career at a tier-two school with limited resources and limited personnel, I have frequently found myself in the position of developing mentoring plans including traditional models, peer mentoring, and group mentoring for faculty. Typical of faculty at this type of intuitions, I am an active researcher in my field, but I also spend considerable time doing teaching and service. I also have had the opportunity to fill administrative positions (chair and associate dean) that I probably would not have had at a top-tiered institution. Serving in these positions has broadened my perspective on my institution.

Finally, like most faculty members in these types of universities, I have stayed where I am because I love my institution and the opportunities it gives me for intense interaction with students and with disparate faculty from very different perspectives and fields that I would probably never interact with were I at a top-tiered institution.

That being said, I also realize there are drawbacks to being in a tier-two institution. Some of these I have experienced firsthand; others I have watched colleagues struggle with. These drawbacks include a lack of resources and the feeling of isolation that results from being the only person in my field of study in my department for much of my career. As both a senior faculty member and a person in administrative positions, I have needed to mentor folks who are not in my field and have had to learn the basic principles of good mentoring on my own.

This book is written for all of you in a similar situation. It assumes you are dedicated. It assumes you truly care about your academic discipline, your institution, and the faculty, the staff, and the students you work with every day. It also assumes you are not trained in faculty development and higher education administration. As such, it is written in a conversational, and occasionally somewhat irreverent, style. It is hoped that this style makes the book more accessible to those not immersed in the higher education administration literature and jargon.

Each chapter contains a fictional case study that might seem a bit over the top to some, but parts of these studies are things we have all experienced to some degree or another at our institutions. There are no easy, one-size-fits-all answers to the issues presented, but there are skills and processes presented that anyone can use and modify to address common issues in mentoring that arise. These processes and skills are developed both through my own experience as a senior faculty member, a department chair, and an associate dean and in a number of other ad hoc leadership positions.

I have also done a fair amount of research into the higher education administration and faculty development research literature, and it underlies much of what is discussed here. I purposely avoid using the language and empirical findings of this literature but do point you in the direction of where you can find more scholarly work if you would like to delve into the issues discussed here in greater depth.

I hope you enjoy, and more importantly find some useful advice in, the book. As you go through it though, I must ask that you remember two things. First, mentoring is a choice, and you cannot make someone participate if they do not want to. That being said, not everyone knows mentoring is a possibility (or that it is a good thing to do), and some perceive asking for help as a sign of weakness. To overcome these barriers, the development of a culture of mentoring at the institution at the highest level that actively engages folks at varying stages of their career is a must. Second, we all need mentoring, including those of us who are in charge.

REFERENCES

Carnegie Classification of Institutions of Higher Education. n.d. "Basic Classification Description." Accessed October 9, 2015. http://carnegieclassifications.iu.edu.

Clark, Burton R. 1987. *The Academic Life: Small Worlds, Different Worlds*. New York: Carnegie Foundation for the Advancement of Teaching.

Chapter One

Mentoring at Small, Resource-Strapped Colleges and Universities

You may be asking yourself, do we really need yet another book on mentoring in higher education? After all, there are scores of very good books out there already dealing with mentoring graduate students and junior faculty as well as advice on being a good dean, associate dean, and department chair. What more could possibly be said?

Unfortunately, however, many of these volumes assume you have considerable budgets for mentoring and the staff to coordinate these efforts; they provide excellent advice on how to coordinate both group and one-on-one mentoring with networks of mentors for staffs and faculties and have programs in administrative professional development for those wishing to move into those roles. They offer excellent suggestions, such as bringing in mentors from other campuses or sponsoring travel to professional meetings. In short, they are written mostly from the perspective of well-funded institutions of higher education with healthy endowments.

Yes, there will be howls of protest regarding recent budget cuts and never having sufficient resources or personnel, and this is true of even the well-funded institutions. These constraints are felt even more intensely at smaller colleges and universities. (Note: I use the terms *college* and *university* interchangeably throughout this volume.) We are speaking, of course, of the second-tier institutions.

The title of second tier is purely descriptive and should not be seen as an insult. Like their counterparts at the flagship institutions, the staffs, faculties, and administrators of second-tier colleges and universities strive to provide excellent educations for their students, engage with their community in meaningful and important ways, and participate in high-quality research and creative activities. Because of constraints on budgets, personnel, and time, they are often understaffed and undersourced.

For example, it is not unusual for faculty members to be the only people in their area of expertise and for them to teach classes in areas only tangentially related to their research area. In fact, they may rarely teach classes related to their specific research. Similarly, staff members may be covering administrative duties for not one but two or three departments. Administration is similarly understaffed, and the office in charge of mentoring (if one exists at all) for the entire institution may be the purview of a single person (sometimes part-time) or expected "other duties" of deans and department chairs.

In both cases, the people doing the mentoring have likely had no training in the process and are trying to do the best they can do with what little resources they have. As a result, mentoring is often underdeveloped or targeted to a very small group where the perceived need is most desperate (e.g., junior faculty members who are in danger of being denied tenure, or short classes for the staff when new processes are introduced).

So what do you do if mentoring activities need to be established or expanded? If you take this on, whether as a concerned senior faculty member, an administrator, or the head of a brand new center for faculty development, this book is written for you. Although specific mentoring methods and techniques differ depending on the individual or group you are trying to help, there is a tool kit you can develop that is broadly applicable and that can help you tailor your activities to increase the effectiveness of your mentoring programs.

The purpose of this book is to help you develop this tool kit and provide some real-world skills that can be fine-tuned to apply to a variety of situations. To demonstrate their usefulness, each chapter contains a case study (sometimes two) demonstrating a common area where mentoring is needed and approaches that can be used to rectify the situation. None of these methods is completely cost-free, unfortunately, but many have minimal cost and rely on the development of systems of peer mentoring and mutual support. As such, the cost is frequently one of time and organizational skill rather than money.

It is important to remember that people are individuals with their own hopes, dreams, aspirations, and career goals, so with two exceptions, there is no method or action that will work in all cases. That is, there are no universal rules (I will get back to those two exceptions to this statement in a minute). No book can give you all possible mentoring issues you might run into and the solutions to all these issues, not even one as big as the multivolume *Encyclopedia Britannica*. Therefore, I do not attempt that here.

Rather, I want to encourage you to understand the underlying constraints the mentee is facing so you can work together to address these constraints and either eliminate them or devise doable ways to get around them given the resources available. For example, it might be ideal to fly a junior faculty member who is the only person in their field of research to another institution and sponsor them for a summer research project with a senior scholar in their field. Unfortunately, this act is beyond the resources of many departments, divisions/schools, and colleges/universities. What can you do instead to help the junior faculty members jump-start their research agendas?

Similarly, a midcareer faculty member may be floundering in her research, teaching, and service after receiving tenure. Should you just write her off as deadwood, or are there things you can do to help her find a new direction and again thrive and contribute? Hint: I argue the latter is the better way to go.

You have a staff member who in the past was a stellar member of the community but is now finding it impossible to keep up with changing computer systems required for him to do his job. Finding the root of the problem and working with him to overcome it both honors his past contributions and opens the door to future success (a much more profitable outcome than either pushing him out of his job or everyone in the department living in misery).

Finally, a new administrator is hired from outside your institution; she comes in with expectations that everything is the same as in her previous institution and therefore the faculty and staff members must just be lazy or obstructionist when they do not immediately jump on board with new plans. Do you suffer in silence until they move on to a new institution, or do you mentor up and educate her on the culture of the campus, constraints of the faculty and staff, and areas of potential for growth?

So let's get to those two exceptions noted earlier. There are, in fact, two universal rules of mentoring.

1. *The goal of mentoring is not to re-create yourself.* Do not assume you know what the hopes, dreams, and aspirations of the person you are trying to help are. These are different for each person. Some people dream of one day becoming the president of a major university; others have no desire to conquer the world but just want to figure out that new computer program. It is your job to help your mentees figure out their short-term and long-term goals and how to achieve them.

2. *You are not the sage on high dispensing wisdom that all others are too dim to see.* Mentoring is not a unidirectional relationship. Rather, it is a partnership in which both you and your mentee bring something to the table. Together you tackle the issues at hand and, at the risk of being called an unrealistic Pollyanna, you both get something out of that relationship. Do not assume your mentees know nothing. Chances are they have thought about the issues and have some ideas but are just having trouble implementing them or seeing them clearly. Working

together, your mentees will gain some new skills and insights, and so will you.

If you get nothing but these two points from the book, it will have been a success. However, there are a few more tools in the tool kit that have worked for educators in the past. Hopefully they will help you as well, so read on.

WHO NEEDS MENTORING ANYWAY?

Before getting to the specifics of mentoring tools, a bit of context is in order. In a world of increasing budget and time constraints in higher education, everyone is constantly facing new challenges. We all know someone who seems to embrace and overcome all new challenges with ease and sails through life with a smile on their face (yes, feel free to grumble and make snarky remarks about those lucky individuals). In reality, however, most of us are constantly challenged, and even those who seem blessed with unlimited talent and luck stumble on occasion.

The flip side of this, of course, is that everyone also sees the solution that evades the rest of us on some issue, even those who think of themselves as always one step behind the curve. In other words, everyone, from the first day "newbie" to the "seen it all, done it all" old-timer, is a potential mentee or mentor. The trick is figuring out the area and time in which we are best placed in one category or the other and acting accordingly.

The fact of this dual side of everyone's personality is the saving grace of mentoring programs and forms the knowledge base in resource-strapped institutions. A successful mentoring program working on a shoestring budget with limited personnel taps into this fact to help staff members, faculty members, and administrators achieve their goals. The role of the coordinator of the mentoring program is to recognize both the challenges and talents of people and hook them up with the right tool or method for them to succeed. This is true for the individual whose sole job is running a university-wide mentoring center (few and far between at resource-strapped institutions) as well as for the concerned senior faculty member, the department chair, the dean, and others in various administrative roles.

That being said, it is important to remember we are dealing with increasingly complex faculties and staffs. Long gone are the days when there are only three types of jobs at colleges and universities: secretaries, tenure/tenure-track faculty members, and administrators (presidents and deans). Even at the smallest institutions there is a proliferation of the types of jobs we have to accomplish and the specialties needed to do them. Sometimes this results in new jobs with different folks in each job title, and sometimes (increasingly frequently) a single individual is required to wear more and more hats.

For example, secretaries and administrative assistants serving one (or multiple) departments are also charged with managing departmental budgets and purchasing systems, aiding the faculty with complex rules of expenditures tied to grants, projecting student enrollments based on the analysis of past trends, and fixing every and all computer problems that arise. Additional staff members are present in colleges as well, all requiring mentoring. They include individuals involved in highly specialized activities such as laboratory managers, financial aid councilors, and specialists in student advising and other student-support roles, community outreach, fund-raising, and the running of the college's offices of the bursar, registrar, and facilities management, and a host of other areas.

Similarly, faculty members are increasingly diverse. Traditional tenure/tenure-track faculty members charged with teaching, research, and service are joined by other types of faculty with different job descriptions. For example, non–tenure-track faculty members, devoted predominately to teaching, are increasingly important members of the college community. These can be full-time, permanent faculty members, part-time (coming in to teach a class or two a semester) members, or short-term positions (such as artist-in-residence or professors-of-practice) housed in a department for only one semester. Additionally, there are faculty members in libraries, archives, and museum positions and research faculty members who live on soft money from grants and contracts. Because the missions of these roles differ so greatly, mentoring has to shift away from traditional models to embrace the diversity.

Administrators are also increasingly diverse and follow very different career paths to arrive at their current positions. In addition to the president, dean, and chair who arise through the faculty ranks, there are administrators and directors of a number of divisions of any college or university, including the university chief financial officer, the registrar, the head of advising, the director of human resources, and the superintendent of facilities management, who rise through the staff ranks. Each of these individuals has highly specialized knowledge concerning the laws, methods, and theoretical basis of their positions. As administrators, however, they also must become specialists in managing people and in mentoring the individuals who report to them.

In other words, colleges and universities are complicated places full of people who need mentoring in highly disparate jobs. Most conscientious people in supervisory or senior positions attempt ad hoc mentoring with little training or tools; sometimes these attempts are successful and sometimes disastrous. Formal mentoring programs, where they exist, have traditionally focused on only the traditional faculty, and in particular the junior faculty preparing for tenure. At many universities and colleges this occurs in an office of one person, or in a situation lacking a mentoring office it is the responsibility of chairs, deans, directors, and others who have been at the institutions for a while and are willing to "show the ropes" to others. Given this, how do we both master this traditional role of mentoring and extend it out to an increasingly heterogeneous staff, faculty, and administrative body? How do you create a culture of mentoring at the institution in which mentoring occurs in every office and department and the tools of mentoring are widely known. Let's look at a case study that illustrates the point.

Dr. Lucy Goodcitizen was tapped by the provost to coordinate the faculty and the staff working in the advising office to implement a new core curriculum at the college. The provost chose her because she believed Goodcitizen had a skill set necessary to accomplish the goal; she is an award-winning teacher and has run a large and very successful research program for many years and thus has experience supervising researchers and coordinating people doing many different tasks needed to reach a research goal.

In implementing the new core curriculum, Goodcitizen worked with both tenure/tenure-track teachers and non–tenure-track teachers charged with revamping their classes to incorporate new learning objectives of the revised core. She also worked with advising staff members who were implementing a new computerized graduation check-out system that ensured students completed the new core requirements in a timely manner.

For the most part, people embraced the project and successfully completed the new tasks. There were problems with implementation with two groups of people, however. The first is a group of non–tenure-track faculty members (most of whom teach at multiple colleges/universities in the area to cobble together a living wage), and the second is a small group of advisors who were having difficulty with the new computer system, resulting in errors in the student's records.

The non–tenure-track teachers did not attend any of the faculty meetings or workshops where the new curriculum was discussed and continued to teach their classes as though nothing changed. As a result, some members of the core-curriculum oversight committee are calling them recalcitrant and obstructionist and demanding they be banned from teaching core classes. The advisors who are having difficulty with the computer system did attend the training sessions (sometimes multiple times) but are still having difficulty; the errors are causing stress for the students and extra work for the other advisors.

Their supervisor wants to fire them. As a result, the situation has blown up in Goodcitizen's face, morale is sinking, and faculty and staff members are claiming mistreatment. Goodcitizen is at a loss for what to do and has tripled her intake of double espressos in an attempt to work late into the night to fix all of the problems by herself.

Who needs mentoring in this instance? Though this volume only deals with faculties, please take the broader view of a mentoring culture for this example. Five individuals or groups in this case study would benefit from mentoring: Goodcitizen, the non-tenure-track faculty members, the core curriculum oversight committee, the troubled advisors, and their supervisor. They do not, however, need the same kind of mentoring. Additionally, although it appears to be simply a matter of another training session for the advisors to solve this immediate issue, this will not solve either the short-term problem of the core curriculum implementation or the longer-term problem of morale, complaints of mistreatment, and miscommunication. Let's go through the issues.

First, Goodcitizen's situation is typical of many individuals who move from one role (traditional faculty member) to another (administrator); they are moved into these positions because of past success in their jobs and the perceived potential for administrative talent. Unfortunately, most universities do not have a way of mentoring and supporting these individuals as they move into administrative positions—rather, we tend to throw them into the deep end of the pool and let them either sink or swim. The result is frustration on all sides, potential failure of the project, and the refusal of the person to take on leadership positions in the future, resulting in the loss of a valuable asset to the university.

The second individual in an administrative role—the advisor's supervisor—is in a similar situation. As with the faculty, staff members are promoted to supervisory and administrative positions because they demonstrate excellence in their current job and others see their potential to take on more responsibility. However, promotion to a new job requires they develop new skills, possibly in totally new areas. They may have great organizational/ managerial skills but need help making the transition to leadership and serving as a supervisor and mentor for individuals in their areas to help each person rise to their full potential. In other words, they (just like Goodcitizen) are in need of mentoring on how to lead and how to mentor.

The third group that needs mentoring in this case study is the non–tenure-track faculty. Part of this situation relates to a need by administrators to understand the differences in the constraints on the life of non–tenure-track and tenure-track faculty. If workshops and meetings are held during the day when non–tenure-track faculty members are teaching or at another of their jobs, the consequences can be serious. First, they do not get the information, and second, due to the reaction of the curriculum committee, the university may lose excellent teachers who care deeply about their students. Additionally, due to feelings of mistreatment, the non–tenure-track faculty members may feel increasingly marginalized and be reluctant to become more involved in the university community. This can occur either because the ban the core curriculum committee wants is put in place or because they feel they are being treated badly and the college does not care about them and their careers.

Therefore, the fourth group—the core curriculum committee—also needs some attention. They may be experts in pedagogy, but if no one has reached out to guide them in effective communication techniques and consensus building, their message will never get out. The final group is the advisors having trouble with the computer system. Simply sending them to the exact same workshop taught in the same way three or four times is not likely to solve the problem. Why does the problem exist? Are there different ways to approach training, that is, are there learning styles that require different types of interactions? Do their talents serve the project and the college better in another role? What are their short-term goals with respect to this project, and how do these fit into the long-term goals of the advising office and them personally? Although this book concentrates on faculties, staff and administrative mentoring is an equally important activity and deserves equal attention.

Obviously, each of these five individuals or groups needs different kinds of mentoring to achieve different things for the project to be successful and for them to be successful in their careers at the college. In other words, a one-size answer does not fit all. Despite these differences, the same five steps should be taken with each, though the results and outcomes of these steps will differ from individual to individual.

1. *Figure out the goal.* Goals can be both short term (the particular problem at hand in the case study: the core curriculum project) and long term (their long-term goals within the university community). Short-term goals may seem more immediate, but they are always imbedded in the long term, and figuring out both can not only solve the immediate problem but also help keep future problems from arising.
2. *Find the strengths.* Everyone has strengths: areas in which they excel, things they are passionate about, and areas that bring value to their lives and to the college. Find those strengths, emphasize them, and use them to achieve both short-term and long-term goals.
3. *Identify the challenges.* Just as everyone has strengths, everyone has areas in which they have difficulty. We cannot figure out how to overcome these difficulties if we do not know what they are. Therefore, identifying the challenges is just as important as finding the strengths.
4. *Inventory the resources.* To figure out how to achieve the goals by emphasizing strengths and resolving challenges, both the mentors and the mentees must figure out what resources (human, electronic, or other) are available.
5. *Make a plan.* Once the goals, strengths, challenges, and resources are identified, put them together in a plan of action and then actually follow the plan.

Exactly how you do this differs with the individual and the goals, and these are discussed in subsequent chapters of this book. Even though you go through the same five steps, the plan will involve very different tools for different individuals. For some goals and individuals, the traditional one-on-one mentoring with a mentor-mentee relationship at set meeting times is appropriate. More commonly, a one-on-many approach is needed where a single mentee has several mentors they can talk to, depending on the goal. However, this is not the only, and in many cases not the most appropriate, mentoring relationship.

Group mentoring in the form of working-group meetings with a recognized leader guiding the process is appropriate for some. In other instances, peer mentoring, where the role of mentor and mentee is fluid and dynamic, being mutually supportive is the key. The point is, one size does not fit all in the mentoring plan. The goal is to provide a tool kit that directors, chairs, deans, and concerned senior members of the college community can use as they help others and themselves, for in small, resource-strapped institutions it is most frequently these individuals who take on the mentoring role. These methods cost little money but do require an investment of time and a choice to be involved. For this investment, the payoff in terms of productivity, community formation, and overall improvement in morale is potentially substantial.

LET'S SUM IT UP

The purpose of this chapter was not only to introduce the book (and justify its existence) but also to set out a context in which both individual mentoring and a culture of mentoring can develop. Every chapter contains at least one fictionalized case study designed to illustrate issues of concern. Additionally, every chapter contains a section summarizing research from scholarly books and journal articles on the topic, as well as a list of references for this research at the end. Because this book is written for individuals who are not trained in institutional research or higher education administration, it presents the information in a conversational and accessible manner, but it is based in the scholarly research cited.

The purpose of this book is to provide a tool kit for mentoring at resource-strapped institutions. It is built on two rules of mentoring and a five-step process that can be implemented to achieve both short-term and long-term goals. As a reminder, the two rules are as follows:

1. The goal of mentoring is not to re-create yourself but to help mentees achieve their own career goals.

2. The mentor is not the sage on high dispensing wisdom all others are too dim to see, so listen to the mentee and establish a dialogue instead of assuming you know the answer.

Keeping these rules in mind, each chapter ends in a section summing up the issues where these five steps are highlighted.

1. Figure out the short-term and long-term goals.
2. Find the strengths.
3. Find the challenges.
4. Identify the resources.
5. Create the plan of action.

Now that we have set the context and discussed the general, let's talk about the specifics.

Chapter Two

Mentoring Tenure-Track Junior Faculty

The transition from graduate student/postdoctoral fellow to new tenure-track assistant professor is a dramatic one, full of changes and adjustments to new roles, responsibilities, expectations, campus cultures, and living situations. Several studies have collected interview data from graduate students and new tenure-track faculty (Bataille and Brown 2006; Eddy and Gaston-Gayles 2008; Kanuka and Marini 2004; Mullen and Forbes 2000; Rice, Sorcinelli, and Austin 2000). These studies demonstrate considerable differences in what graduate students anticipate life as an assistant professor will be like and what it actually is; the result, frequently, is disillusionment, frustration, and considerable stress. Luckily, there is substantial literature available to senior faculty and administrators who want to help junior faculty make this transition.

Common themes emerge from many of the studies that have been undertaken to understand the issues faced by junior faculty. As individuals move from the role of student and junior partner in the research endeavor to teacher and leader of research projects, they have a base of skills they can build upon but need to rapidly develop new ones. This process is hindered as new faculty members must not only form new support networks for themselves (and frequently their families/spouses/partners) in a new town but also adjust to a new campus culture. This adjustment runs from the everyday (where is the library and where can I get a decent cup of coffee) to the abstract (what is the nature of the political structure in my department, school/division, or college/university, and what are the criteria by which I am evaluated for tenure and for yearly activities).

Because most PhD and postdoctoral programs are tied to well-funded, top-tiered research institutions, this adjustment can be even more difficult as new faculty members move into second- and third-tier institutions with poor-ly supported (or no) graduate programs, out-of-date laboratories, libraries that struggle to pay their yearly subscription bills to professional journals, and little to no travel and research money. The natural sense of isolation and lack of community that occurs when someone moves to a new job and a new town is intensified when they realize they moved from a large research team to a program where they are the only one in their area of expertise.

In situations where multiple fields are put together in a single department (e.g., the department of cultural studies or the department of earth studies), the new faculty member may be the only individual in their academic disci-pline. Although this can lead to increased interdisciplinary research, it can have a negative impact as well. Contributing to the problem is a fear of asking for help or even knowing whom to ask. The following case study illustrates.

For the past five years, Dr. Newbie has been ensconced in a PhD program where he worked with a cohort of eight other students on a well-funded research project directed by the top researcher in his field. It is an exciting and intellectually stimulating time: they are getting wonderful results, lunch-time brown-bag lectures by top scholars are common, and discussions of method and theory and the latest research in the field dominate get-togethers on the weekends and at night. Newbie works hard and emerges from this experience with a newly minted PhD, inclusion as a coauthor on half a dozen articles, and after successful interviews at his professional meetings and on campus, a new job as an assistant professor at Middle Country University.

Newbie packs up and moves to his new home and eagerly awaits the start of the fall semester. During the move, the chair of his new department sends him an e-mail telling him that he has been assigned a master's-level seminar in his area, as well as an introductory course (along with a course release for his first semester), on the assumption these would be the two easiest classes to start with. Additional good news is that space in a research lab has opened up on campus that Newbie can share with another researcher, but he needs to think about what equipment he will need to stock his portion of the lab for his research so they can strategize on where he should submit a grant proposal to pay for the equipment. Slightly overwhelmed but optimistic and excited, Newbie starts working on his syllabi and looks forward to the start of the semester.

The week before class starts, Newbie does an inventory and finds his lab mate congenial, though in a completely different field with different lab needs; the lab space he has is small but adequate, and he begins to make lists of what he needs so he can talk with the chair about possible funding sources. On the first day of class, however, he is shocked to find one hundred students in his introductory class with more asking to get in; those extra papers he assigned the students on the syllabus are starting to worry him, especially after he finds out there is no money for a student teaching assistant or grader. His graduate seminar is a more manageable with twenty students, but he quickly finds many of the students do not have the background he assumed, and he has to radically rethink how the class is structured. Despite this restructuring, the student complaints about the workload are loud and continuous to both Newbie and his department chair.

Four months later Newbie has survived the first semester, but he spent so much time getting his classes up and running smoothly he has not even started to think about where to submit grant proposals, much less writing them for the needed lab equipment, and his research is at a standstill. Further, the idea of teaching three classes in the spring (even if the introductory class is already prepared) is causing him to hyperventilate, and he is wondering if coming to Middle Country University was the biggest mistake of his life. At the moment, all he can think of is sleeping for three days straight and then going to his professional meetings where he can talk to people about research without explaining basic concepts. In short, Newbie is tired, a little frustrated, and feeling overwhelmed and a bit isolated.

Newbie's experiences are not unusual but, if left unchecked, could grow into disillusionment and the potential loss of a faculty member. When trying to figure out what to do to help Newbie adjust to his new academic home, the senior faculty and administrators of his department and university must first understand the challenges he faces (challenges they themselves faced long ago but have probably forgotten). Once they understand these, they can move to creating a mentoring structure that supports Newbie and allows him to flourish.

REALITIES OF LIFE AS AN ASSISTANT PROFESSOR

New faculty members, particularly those straight from PhD and postdoctoral programs at large, well-funded research institutions, are used to succeeding, especially in the area of research, which has been the major focus of their energy in recent years. They expect similar levels of productivity of themselves as they move into the faculty ranks and experience considerable stress and frustration when they run into difficulties. Many refrain from asking for help because they are afraid it makes them look unqualified or inadequate or they ask for resources that were common at the large, well-funded research university where they received their PhD and are shocked to find they are absent at their new academic home.

Additionally, many are unsure where they should concentrate their efforts. Despite past success in research, they now find themselves in a different role. Moreover, many have little or no teaching experience and have difficulty with basic tasks of constructing syllabi, determining the appropriate level of work for undergraduate classes, and managing classroom dynamics.

In the realm of teaching there are additional issues they probably never thought about, including students who are taking the class only because it is required and are not motivated to work hard. Plus, issues of academic dishonesty arise that new assistant professors never dreamed of committing when they were undergraduates and that completely flabbergast them now they are instructors. Added to concerns of research and teaching is the brand-new phenomenon of university service.

There have been a number of studies looking at the life of junior faculty, including both large-scale surveys and smaller focus groups. For those of you who are numbers averse, do not panic. This book summarizes the data using words instead of statistical formulas. For those of you who love data, check out the cited references.

Based on interviews with ninety-six assistant professors at eight different public universities, Katherine O'Connor and colleagues (2011) argue that most junior faculty members feel tension between spending time on research and time on teaching. Unable to find a balance, assistant professors push themselves harder and harder, and many end up working eighty hours a week, eliminating any downtime and thus having negative impacts on both their personal lives and their health (see similar results in the following studies: Eddy and Gaston-Gayles 2008; Rice et al. 2000; Smith et al. 2001; and Sorcinelli 1994).

This stress is further exacerbated when it is unclear what the department or institution values or when statements about what is valued do not match what is rewarded in annual reviews or the tenure process. For example, although all institutions of higher learning state they value teaching, analysis of the data suggest they do not actually reward it. James Fairweather (2005) used data from surveys completed by more than seventeen thousand faculty members as part of the National Survey of Post-Secondary Faculty in 1992–1993 and 1998–1999. In both sets of data, salary was negatively related to the number of hours spent in the classroom, regardless of the type of institution.

In other words, as the number of hours spent in the classroom went up, salary went down, and the relationship held not only for tier-one research universities but also at tier-two (and tier-three) institutions. Conversely, pay was positively related to number of publications at all institution types. The problem is, of course, that teaching is where new faculty members tend to have the least experience and therefore spend the most time trying to master in their first few years. Further, they are told it is important and valued, but frequently it is not rewarded.

More in-depth interviews and focus group studies demonstrate that junior faculty members are very much aware of this relationship, and it is a source of frustration for many (Eddy and Gaston-Gayles 2008; Rice et al. 2000; Smith et al. 2001; Sorcinelli 1994). The result is the tension between teaching and research noted above and an inability to find a work-life balance as the workload seems to never decrease. Clearly, the data indicate new faculty members are struggling with unrealistic expectations of what they can accomplish and in finding solutions on how to balance the various aspects of their job and life.

Given this, you may ask why they don't just ask for help and let someone know they are struggling. The answer to this question is multifaceted, but at least part of the issue is they do not know whom to ask. Different universities have different cultures and different structural organizations; these are the unwritten rules of interaction that junior faculty members do not know about unless someone points them out or they unwittingly break them. Before new faculty members can figure out where to ask for help, they have to figure out these new cultures and structures. It is the responsibility of the senior faculty and administrators to help them to do this. Let's look a little more closely at each of the areas new faculty members have to balance.

Transitioning from Student to Teacher

Teaching is one of the areas new faculty members struggle with the most (Baldwin 1990; Mullen and Forbes 2000). Few doctoral programs train their students in teaching (Eddy and Gaston-Gayles 2008), and experience may be restricted to having been a teaching assistant or possibly the instructor of a class or two in their area. Rarely, however, have they taught multiple new-class preparations at once and almost never classes outside their areas of expertise.

Additionally, universities have different policies and rules about syllabus construction, learning outcomes, assessments, and benchmarks for students (especially for classes in the university-wide core). New faculty members will be unfamiliar with these, and senior faculty members tend to be so used to or enmeshed in these rules they do not think about others being unfamiliar with the protocols. In other words, even at the most basic level, senior faculty members and administrators need to be purposeful and proactive in reaching out to junior faculty members and not assuming they have experience or knowledge before asking.

Even if new faculty members are given and master information on course mechanics specific to their new institutions, there are other areas with which they have no experience. Although most students are hardworking and take their studies seriously, they have complicated lives, similar to our own. Many students work, some have families, and they have to balance the demands of school, work, and life. Even those students who are full-time, without having to work and worry over family issues, must balance the demands of multiple classes and other student cocurricular activities.

Many new faculty members are shocked to find students who do not put their class as their first priority because of this balancing act. Additionally, there is the small percentage of students who are simply not interested in the subject matter and treat the class as a requirement to get out of the way with the least amount of effort to get the result they want.

Another situation difficult for new faculty members is the small percentage of students who are disruptive or who plagiarize or cheat and then challenge the faculty members' penalty, even while admitting to the offense. At the end of the semester, new faculty members may encounter that small proportion of students who, upon receiving anything less than an A, will threaten to sue, call the dean or university president to complain, or simply show up in the faculty member's office crying and begging for additional work that would allow for a change of grade after the fact.

Even if the new faculty member has wonderful students who are fascinated by the topic, would never dream of cheating, and would never use their teacher as a scapegoat for their performance, there are other areas where new faculty members may need help. First, because new faculty members have been so immersed in the research of their field of study for some time, they may have difficulty calculating where to pitch their classes (as was the case with Newbie for his graduate seminar in our case study).

The result is either a course that assumes the students have considerably more prior knowledge of the subject than they do (the "everyone knows that" syndrome) or subject matter that is made so basic the course does not challenge and completely bores the students (the "dumb it down" syndrome). The result is frustration for both the new faculty member and the students. Unfortunately, the faculty member may not see the full extent of the students' frustration until after the semester is over, when student evaluations of their classes are released. The negative reviews are just one more blow to the confidence of struggling faculty members who are used to success and do not understand what they are doing wrong.

As a result, student evaluations are a source of feedback, and new faculty members are likely to need the help of a senior faculty member to interpret and use the results to improve their classes. It is a considerable shock the first time they receive an evaluation with a statement such as, "The best way to improve this class is to fire the instructor," with no specifics on where the issues may lie. In interviews with first- and second-year faculty members, Robert Boice (1991) found low teaching evaluations were common for new teachers and a source of concern for most; the concern is multifold.

As noted above, new faculty members are used to success, especially in research. But teaching is a different set of skills, and they may be shocked by negative evaluations and take them as an indication that students do not like them personally rather than an indication that there are new skills they need to acquire or improve.

In recent years, student evaluations have moved beyond reports to the faculty members themselves or possible publication on their campus into very public formats like RateMyProfessor.com that publishes results nationwide. The negative impact of bad evaluations in these very public forums on the new faculty member's confidence is considerable. This is in keeping with modern culture's emphasis on social media (think of the popularity of Yelp.com and its use by many to pick the best restaurant or hotel). It introduces an extra level of pressure and fear of public humiliation for new faculty members that senior faculty members did not face early in their careers.

Unfortunately, interviews also demonstrated most new faculty members have difficulty interpreting the results and implementing changes in their class to address them. Rather, they became more nervous, more cautious, and more conservative, and tended to fall back on a lecture format dominated by stating one fact after another rather than engaging the students in new and different ways. Some possible ways senior faculty members and administrators can help struggling teachers are offered in the solution section of this chapter. But first, it is important to look at the challenges tied to research faced by new faculty members.

Changing Role from Team Member to Leader in Research and Creative Activities

Because new faculty members have been extensively trained in the method and theory of their fields and actively pursued a research agenda to produce their PhD dissertation and possibly postdoctoral research, many institutions, as well as the new faculty members themselves, assume they need no help in this area. As a result, many institutions that do have formal mentoring programs for junior faculty members or centers for faculty development concentrate exclusively on teaching (Jarvis 1992).

In contrast to this response by institutions, however, studies that have conducted in-depth interviews with junior faculty members demonstrate the struggle they have in the area of research and the junior faculties' explicit statements about needing help in the area of research and creative activities (Mullen and Forbes 2000; O'Connor et al. 2011). Some of these struggles relate to time pressures noted above and highlighted in the case study.

Time constraint is not the only issue that came to the fore in the interviews, however. Specifically, new faculty members have come from situations where they have a mentor to help them think strategically about research or creative projects, where to apply for grants, or the best peer-re-viewed/juried venues to submit their work (Eddy and Gaston-Gayles 2008). Additionally, their cohort of fellow students and researchers or artists served as a ready-made sounding board and a peer group to critique manuscripts and creative works.

Based on extensive interviews with thirty-eight assistant professors at two different universities, O'Connor and colleagues note that "respondents repeatedly mentioned wanting a mentor to assist with developing a line of research, publishing manuscripts, obtaining grants and achieving tenure" (2011, 6). This is particularly true for faculty members whose research and creative activities require substantial financial resources as external funding becomes increasingly difficult to obtain.

Faculty members at second-tier institutions are in competition for those increasingly limited dollars with more established researchers at top-tiered institutions with well-staffed offices of sponsored research including grant writers, people to help search for funding, and experts in navigating complicated submission systems. On their own, new faculty members attempt several strategies to dealing with difficulties in their research agendas. For example, they may take on smaller, local projects with limited impact that require little funding. Alternatively, they may restrict their submissions to regional or local venues (with high acceptance rates and therefore low impact factors) for dissemination of their work to ensure some publications or juried works for their tenure dossiers.

Finally, they may fall back on their networks from graduate school rather than developing new collaborators and projects that would demonstrate independence. All three can have a negative impact on achieving tenure due to the inability to demonstrate a positive impact on the field and the establishment of independence. Even if faculty members are successful in their quest for tenure using this strategy, it can have the consequence of increasing feelings of professional/scholarly isolation as they rely on collaborations and networks that are outside of the university community they now inhabit.

The isolation many junior faculty members feel at their new institution is particularly acute in the area of research at smaller, resource-strapped institutions because they often are the only person in their area of expertise in their department. Even if this is not the case, however, feelings of isolation can occur. In fact, the lack of a "community of scholars" that provides both intellectual stimulation and a social support system is a recurrent theme in interviews with junior faculty members (Bataille and Brown 2006; Kanuka and Marini 2004; O'Meara, Terosky, and Neumann 2008; Ponjuan, Conley, and Trower 2011; Rice et al. 2000; Sorcinelli 1994). These same studies demonstrate that feeling as though you are a part of a community and collaborations with colleagues on different types of projects (teaching or research) is a major source of job satisfaction.

Given that we know this, why do junior faculty members feel so isolated even in departments where there are others doing similar research? In some cases it is simply a matter of time. As we discuss in the next chapter, time constraints do not disappear after tenure; rather, the source of time conflict just shifts, and associate professors also struggle to find balance. A second reason may be differences in research orientation and methodology or differing comfort levels with new technologies between junior and senior faculty members (see chapter 4).

Finally, midcareer and senior faculty members may feel some ambivalence toward junior faculty members who are now competing with them for the same limited pool of resources and who received start-up packages that were not available to earlier generations of the faculty. Regardless of the cause, junior faculty members cite the lack of collegiality as a major source of dissatisfaction, and senior faculty members and administrators need to be mindful of its impact.

Groups with Additional Issues that Need to Be Considered

Beyond the issues discussed above, faculty members from underrepresented minorities and women (especially women in STEM [science, technology, engineering, and mathematics] fields) face additional roadblocks that need to be remembered. Specifically, both conscious and unconscious bias exist against faculty members of color and women in the area of research, teaching, and service. For junior faculty, these issues can exacerbate and escalate the problems that exist with making the transition from student to faculty member. These issues are discussed in detail in chapter 7.

DEVELOPING MENTORING RELATIONSHIPS THROUGH MULTIPLE MEANS

As noted in chapter 1, one size does not fit all. That being said, not every issue requires a one-on-one meeting to determine goals, skills, and plans of actions. It is important for those of us who have been at the institution for a while to remember that not everyone has the institutional memory we have. When we fulfill policy requirements or contact the appropriate office to aid in completion of a task, we forget that not everyone, especially among new faculty members, has that knowledge base.

For example, not every institution has a syllabus policy and defined learning outcomes for classes taught in the university-wide core, and those that do differ from university to university. If a new faculty member comes from an institution with no policy or if they have never taught a core class, they would not even know to ask about required procedures. Additionally, if no one has talked to them about assessment practices in a context relevant to their classes, they may assume their final grades are sufficient assessment tools. In terms of research, new faculty members will not automatically know whom to contact to find out about required overhead to be added to their budget or how to obtain a course release tied to a grant. Further, they may not know how to submit grant proposals at their new academic home.

Much of the faculty information about whom to contact for specific activities and policies can be handled in an orientation session with handouts that the new faculty can keep for future reference. Similarly, small working groups led by experienced teachers are good for new teachers to help them figure out how to meet university requirements while still maintaining the academic freedom and creativity crucial for good teaching. Likewise, group discussions with faculty members of all ranks within a content area can bring to light not only the importance to administrators and accreditors of assessment but also the usefulness of assessment exercises to better understand student comprehension of practical issues and skills by the faculty member teaching the class. Finally, a periodic query of "how are you doing?" or "any questions on anything?" by a senior faculty member can open the door for improved mentoring. This last action, with its personal touch, is particularly important, because personalities of the new faculty members we are trying to help vary so considerably.

We know from study after study that all new faculty members benefit from mentoring relationships (Baldwin 1990; Kanuka and Marini 2004; Mullen and Forbes 2000; O'Connor et al. 2011; Pifer and Baker 2013; Sorcinelli 1994). These benefits range from helping decode the institutional culture and rules to developing new skills in time management, networking, building collaborations, dealing with classroom issues, and improving their teaching. Not all new faculty members need the same kind or level of mentoring, however, due to differences in their graduate preparation (Eddy and Gaston-Gayles 2008; Rice et al. 2000) and personality (Dowd and Kaplan 2005; Pifer and Baker 2013).

If when checking in with a new faculty member you discover there is an issue beyond basic factual information, determining the nature of the problem is frequently far from straightforward, and you may have to dig a bit deeper. "I'm having trouble with research" can have numerous sources ranging from "I need someone to bounce ideas off of" to "I'm not sure where to submit an article or creative work"; "I would like collaborators but am having trouble developing them"; and "my research is held up because I'm missing a crucial piece of equipment." A similar range of possible statements can arise from the declaration "I'm having trouble with teaching."

Two studies (Dowd and Kaplan 2005; Pifer and Baker 2013) argue that the first step in helping new faculty members define their specific problem (and therefore find a solution) is to understand their personalities. At one level, this is understanding basic personalities in terms of a series of continuums (e.g., introvert/extrovert, risk averse/risk embracing, and high self-confidence/low self-confidence), their view of the institution (I'm part of the structure vs. I'm an autonomous scholar who happens to work here), and differing skill sets (political awareness and communication). Though they concentrate on different aspects, both studies developed similar classifications of faculty that are useful to understanding the different mentoring strategies that senior faculty members and administrators can deploy.

At its simplest iteration, you can think of new faculty members on a continuum with two types of people at the extremes. Rarely are the extremes of the continuum met perfectly, and most people are somewhere in between, but understanding the range of variation is instructive.

At one end of the continuum (type A) are individuals who see their primary allegiance to the institution rather than their field of study. These individuals are interested in putting down roots and hope to stay at the same place their entire career. On the positive side, they tend to be very aware of political connections and are concerned with maintaining an image of collegiality and helpfulness. They make good collaborators and are often comfortable in group settings but feel isolated in their research if they are the only one in their field of study and are hesitant to take risks because they lack connections in their field to talk about possible benefits of those risks. Further, they may be afraid to ask for help because it makes them look unqualified.

At the other end of the continuum (type B), faculty members define themselves primarily through their discipline, and maybe department, rather than their institution. On the positive side, they tend to have a great deal of self-confidence, are not afraid to take risk in their research, and are not afraid to ask for resources or information. They tend to be self-directed but are not good at making connections with others at their institutions; they are frequently introverts and often feel isolated and lonely. Although they may have good connections with scholars in their research fields at other institutions, they have difficulty making connections with others at their own institution, including students.

These two types of individuals have very different skills upon which to build. Conversely, the areas where they need help and the types of resources they will find helpful are very different. Type A individuals often struggle to get their research going, either because they get so involved in teaching and service they lack time or because they don't know how to break into new areas, start new projects, or find individuals to hash out new ideas and get feedback on early drafts of manuscripts. Type B personalities, on the other hand, have difficulty making connections with students and with faculty members in other areas of specialization. This is particularly difficult at smaller, resource-strapped institutions where they are the only individual in their area of specialization.

Possible Solutions and Courses of Action:
Kick-Starting the Research

In helping type A individuals kick-start their research, the most profitable solution is to build on their strengths of collaboration and connection. Specifically, the formation of peer-mentoring groups often works better with this type of individual than traditional one-on-one mentoring, especially in terms of research. Cross-departmental group mentoring expands the network type A faculty members can tap into and provides networks that may start as support systems and evolve into interdisciplinary partners (Kanuka and Marini 2004; Smith et al. 2001; Zachary and Fischer 2009).

The role of senior faculty members in these arrangements is to help match people of similar needs and interest, as well as the logistics of getting folks together in one place at one time, rather than to formally direct them. For example, a group concentrating on the historical sciences may include physicists, geologists, anthropologists, and biologists; a group concerned with environmental issues may include geographers, chemists, ecologists, and meteorologists; and a group concerned with urban issues may include city planners, sociologists, criminologists, and public health scholars.

These combinations may seem obvious when written on the page, but junior faculty members who don't know the institution or faculty members outside their own department and generally see their research in terms of the department structure in which they received their degrees may not think of this possibility. If a junior faculty member does think of this, they do not know who these individuals are at their new institution. Even if these interactions do not lead to research collaborations, just having someone to talk about research with and to bounce ideas off of can help lessen feelings of isolation.

These groups work best when they decide their own agenda, they meet frequently (say once a week for a brown bag), and everyone is seen as an equal participant rather than a senior faculty member directing a seminar group. That being said, there is a role for senior faculty members in these groups. They serve both as a source of information about resources and as the person who can provide logistical/organizational support. In terms of the latter, sending an e-mail out to find a time when everyone can meet and locating a room to meet in can benefit struggling junior faculty members way beyond the time it takes the senior faculty members to organize the meeting.

First, it demonstrates someone at the institution cares and is willing to invest in the faculty member, and second, the resulting discussion can spark the kind of creative atmosphere the junior scholar felt in graduate school. The meetings should be kept informal, however, without rank distinctions. Participants should pick the priorities, which may range from reading groups comparing theories and methods that are complementary in related fields, sounding boards for new ideas or working out problems in methodology, and strategies for picking the best outlet to disseminate research and creative works.

It is crucial they meet on a regular schedule. Not only does this provide a set meeting schedule that time-crunched faculty members can count on, but also it gives the deadline-driven members of the group the structure they need to produce results. That is, the deadline-driven members of the group (and let's face it, that is most of us) are less likely to put off working on research if they know someone in their monthly or weekly research group is going to ask them specifically what they have worked on since the last meeting. This can be reinforced if different group members take the lead each meeting or if there is an expectation that drafts of articles will be circulated prior to the meeting for feedback. Scholars in the humanities have long used these types of arrangements as writing groups that critique each other's work and help ready it for submission or for preparing book proposals, and they can easily be expanded to other fields.

Possible Solutions and Courses of Action: Improving Teaching

Type B faculty members are often good at maintaining networks with other researchers in their field electronically and through professional conferences, workshops, and juried festivals but lack connections on campus. Because engaging with others on a daily basis is not their strong suit, they often do better with a one-on-one mentoring relationship and with concentrating on connections within their own departments to strengthen their ties to the institution and, in particular, to their students.

Interviews indicate that having a "point person" in their department they can go to for advice and information is of primary concern for type B faculty members (Kanuka and Marini 2004; O'Connor et al. 2011). Because the difficulty of making connections often manifests itself in teaching, this is often the most immediate area of need. The development of programs of reciprocal class visits often helps. Specifically, senior faculty members known for their expertise in teaching can offer to sit in on classes the new faculty members are struggling with to offer explicit feedback that can then be implemented.

Alternatively, junior faculty members can be asked to sit in on a senior faculty member's class to see successful teaching methods in action. If a pattern is evident in teaching evaluations, such as organization and engaging students, these visits can be coordinated to concentrate on these issues. Additionally, exchange and critique of syllabi and rubrics may help. It is important that senior faculty members approach the junior faculty members with an attitude of mutual support and exchange of ideas rather than as an evaluation or mandatory remediation when setting up these relationships. As such, the earlier it is done in the career of the junior faculty member the better. The combination of external networks and pairing with more senior faculty members in their own or closely related departments has been found to be one of the most effective mentoring methods for type B faculty members (Mullen and Forbes 2000).

LET'S SUM IT UP

Let's sum up by relating this discussion back to the steps we outlined in chapter 1. Because junior faculty members are making such a huge transition, going from student/postdoctoral researcher to faculty member and usually from a large, well-funded research university to a smaller resource-challenged institution, it is tempting to say that the *goal* is tenure and that they need help with everything. In reality, their needs for mentoring generally fall into three defined areas: (1) learning the culture and policies of their new institution, (2) establishing an independent research/creative agenda, and (3) developing teaching skills for a variety of class types and varying levels of student preparedness.

Almost all junior faculty members need help with goal 1, but usually they don't need help beyond basic resources and policy information and the occasional checking in with by the senior faculty member. Generally, new faculty members, depending on their personalities, need more help in either goal 2 or 3 but not necessarily both. Understanding this allows senior faculty members to tailor their mentoring to concentrate more heavily on one or the other.

Both the *challenges* junior faculty members face and the *strengths* they bring to the table are related to each other and vary depending on their graduate school preparation and their personalities. Some junior faculty members need help primarily in the area of research and creative activities, and cross-department peer groups with related interests are often the ideal mechanism for mentoring. Other junior faculty members need help making connections with their colleagues and students, and more traditional one-on-one mentoring models work well. The key to creating a *plan* of action is figuring out where the junior faculty needs help and, based on their personalities, the best way to provide that help.

REFERENCES

Baldwin, Roger G. 1990. "Faculty Career Stages and Implications for Professional Development." In *Enhancing Faculty Careers: Strategies for Development and Renewal*, edited by Jack H. Schuster and Daniel W. Wheeler, 20–40. San Francisco: Jossey-Bass.

Bataille, Gretchen, and Betsy E. Brown. 2006. *Faculty Career Paths: Multiple Routes to Academic Success and Satisfaction*. Westport, CT: Praeger.

Boice, Robert. 1991. "New Faculty as Teachers." *Journal of Higher Education* 62 (2): 150–73.

Dowd, Karen O., and David M. Kaplan. 2005. "The Career Life of Academics: Boundaried or Boundaryless?" *Human Relations* 58 (6): 699–721.

Eddy, Pamela L., and Joy L. Gaston-Gayles. 2008. "New Faculty on the Block: Issues of Stress and Support." *Journal of Human Behavior in the Social Environment* 17 (1–2): 89–106.

Fairweather, James Steven. 2005. "Beyond the Rhetoric: Trends in the Relative Value of Teaching and Research in Faculty Salaries." *Journal of Higher Education* 76 (4): 401–22.

Jarvis, Donald K. 1992. "Improving Junior Faculty Scholarship." *New Directions for Teaching and Learning* 50: 63–72.

Kanuka, Heather, and Anthony Marini. 2004. "Empowering Untenured Faculty through Mosaic Mentoring." *Canadian Journal of University Continuing Education* 30 (2): 11–38.

Mullen, Carol A., and Sean A. Forbes. 2000. "Untenured Faculty: Issues of Transition, Adjustment and Mentorship." *Mentoring and Tutoring* 8 (1): 31–46.

O'Connor, Katherine, H. Carol Greene, Amy J. Good, and Guili Zhang. 2011. "Finding Balance: A Challenge for Untenured Faculty." *International Education Studies* 4 (4): 3–12.

O'Meara, Kerry Ann, Aimee LaPointe Terosky, and Anna Neumann. 2008. *Faculty Careers and Worklives*. ASHE Higher Education Report 34, no. 3. San Francisco: Jossey-Bass.

Pifer, Meghan J., and Vicki L. Baker. 2013. "Managing the Process: The Intradepartmental Networks of Early-Career Academics." *Innovative Higher Education* 38: 323–37.

Ponjuan, Luis, Valerie Martin Conley, and Cathy Trower. 2011. "Career Stage Differences in Pre-Tenure Track Faculty Perceptions of Professional and Personal Relationships with Colleagues." *Journal of Higher Education* 82 (3): 319–46.

Rice, R. Eugene, Mary Deane Sorcinelli, and Ann E. Austin. 2000. *Heeding New Voices: Academic Careers for a New Generation*. Washington, DC: American Association for Higher Education.

Smith, Judith Osgood, Joy S. Whitman, Peggy A. Grant, Annette Stanutz, J. A. Russett, and Karon Rankin. 2001. "Peer Networking as a Dynamic Approach to Supporting New Faculty." *Innovative Higher Education* 25:197–207.

Sorcinelli, Mary Deane. 1994. "Effective Approaches to New Faculty Development." *Journal of Counseling and Development* 72: 474–79.

Zachary, Lois J., and Lori A. Fischer. 2009. *The Mentee's Guide*. San Francisco: Jossey-Bass.

Chapter Three

Mentoring Midcareer Faculty

Life between Tenure and Promotion to Full Professor

When institutions have limited funds for mentoring programs, they are generally concentrated on junior faculty members making their way toward tenure. At one level, this is understandable; tenure is an up-or-out decision in most places, so the stakes are very high. After tenure, however, faculty members move into a whole new world in which they are expected to shift overnight from protected and mentored junior faculty members to midcareer faculty members who carry the bulk of the service obligations for the department and university, and deal with a lack of clear institutional benchmarks and no formal mentoring. The results are high levels of dissatisfaction and disillusionment (Hagedorn 2000; Strage and Merdinger 2014; Wilson 2012). Given this, what can concerned senior faculty members, department chairs, deans, provosts, and the midcareer faculty members themselves do? A case study illustrates the situation.

Dr. Early Star was very excited to receive a letter from the president of the university at the end of the spring semester informing him that he had been awarded tenure and promoted to associate professor. He spread the word and planned a celebration for later that evening. Later that day, the current chair of Star's department (Dr. Burnedout) came into his office to congratulate him on receiving tenure. This congratulations was followed by the statement that Burnedout's second term as chair ends at the end of the semester.

Of the other tenured members of the department, two were counting down to retirement and one would spend the next year on a Fulbright-sponsored sabbatical out of the country. Therefore, Star would need to take over as chair effective at the end of the semester. Although Star would have preferred to follow his tenure decision with a sabbatical of his own, he realizes he had been protected as a junior faculty member and it was "his turn" to chair.

Star dived into his new chair responsibilities with gusto: mentoring and protecting the junior faculty; mediating conflicts among the senior faculty; dealing with student petitions and complaints; and attending endless meetings of committees and subcommittees. This was accompanied by ongoing teaching responsibilities (the position came with a single course release) as well as mentoring and advising individual students.

Star continued to publish, using existing data for the first two years of his three-year term. Unfortunately, by year three he was out of data and had not had time to start a new project since receiving tenure, so the lack of publications was likely to continue for a few more years. Despite his outstanding service/administration and teaching, he received a low evaluation score his third year as chair because he did not publish or submit any new grant proposals.

As Star thinks about the future and his desire to be promoted to full professor, he starts to take stock. He has been so busy with administrative and service work to his department and university that he turned down requests to serve on committees for his disciplinary societies for the last three years. Additionally, his university has limited travel funds for all but the junior faculty members, so he only attends his professional meetings when he is presenting a paper, which he has not done in the last two years. Finally, since colleagues at other, larger, institutions have not seen him at the annual meetings or served with him on professional committees, they did not think to include him in a new multi-institution collaborative project (i.e., out of sight out of mind). In other words, Star is good and truly stuck and not sure what to do to get unstuck.

Unfortunately, Star's predicament is all too common (and is probably the source of Burnedout's fate as well). One of the great ironies of our profession is that the least amount of mentoring and resources are available for the largest segment of the tenure/tenure-track faculty members of a university and for the biggest portion of a faculty member's career. As noted above, this is partly driven by the need to use the limited funds available for faculty development on junior faculty members preparing for tenure.

There is also the belief that midcareer faculty members should have "figured it out by now." The problem is, of course, the type of mentoring they need as a newly tenured faculty member is not the same as what they needed as a junior faculty member—what they figured out was how to get tenure, not what is next. Faculty members can spend very long periods of time as associate professors, but their lives and the issues they are dealing with are considerably different from junior faculty members and will shift through the midcareer phase (see Baldwin 1990 for a detailed discussion of this). What can be done? What advice and tools can concerned senior faculty members and administrators provide to associate professors to keep them engaged in all three areas (research, teaching, and service) and to help jump-start them in areas where they have started to falter?

REALITIES OF LIFE AS AN ASSOCIATE PROFESSOR

It is important to start this discussion with an understanding of what life is like for associate professors. Everyone's circumstances are a bit different, of course, but there have been some recent studies indicating consistent issues that midcareer faculty members must deal with. (Yes, this is where I throw a bunch of data at you.) For those of you who like numbers, check out the cited works for more detail.

There have been some recent surveys of midcareer faculty members that show some interesting and consistent results. Some of these involve a small sample of faculty members at a single institution using in-depth interviews (Buch et al. 2011; Neumann and Terosky 2007), and others are based on standardized questionnaires on a very large sample of faculty members, often from multiple institutions (Baldwin, Lunceford, and Vanderlinden 2005; Wilson 2012). Consistently, results indicate increasing amounts of time spent on service and administration after tenure.

The amount of time spent teaching remains approximately the same. The result is time pulled away from research programs to accommodate the increasing service demand. This time squeeze occurs at the same point of life when personal and family demands may be at their height (i.e., children, aging parents, health issues of faculty members themselves or their spouse, etc.). The result is high levels of dissatisfaction and frustration that there is insufficient time to stay current in their field of study, much less be innovative (see Baldwin et al. 2005 in particular for a comprehensive analysis).

As faculty members progress further into midcareer, boredom may increase a sense of dissatisfaction as the exact same classes are taught year after year, yet another round of budget cuts is announced, and committee work seems to continue in perpetuity with no tangible results (I know, I know, I am sounding incredibly gloomy, but I am just telling you the study results—it is the perception of many associate professors). Here is the second bit of irony, however. The survey data indicate that despite these frustrations, midcareer is also the most productive time of an academic's research career on several measures. So what is going on?

Roger Baldwin (1990) and his colleagues (Baldwin et al. 2008; Baldwin et al. 2005; see also O'Meara, Terosky, and Neumann 2008) have probably spent more time looking at this issue than anyone else. Pulling from theoretical work in life-cycle analysis and developmental psychology, Baldwin argues that we need to think of midcareer as a dynamic time characterized by periods of high levels of productivity interspersed every five to seven years with periods of monotony, boredom, uncertainty about the future, and self-doubt in which productivity plateaus. Not everyone goes through these cycles, but most people do. Unfortunately, not everyone emerges from the research plateau back into a cycle of research productivity without some help.

For those that do not, they may end up with disillusionment and either leave the academy or become the infamous "deadwood" we all know and fret over. It is these periods of plateau where mentoring is most needed. The post-tenure slump experienced by Dr. Early Star in our first case study is one of these. After seven years at his university, he moved from a goal-oriented (i.e., tenure) period as an assistant professor into a new phase where additional service and removal from the research-active environment of professional meetings resulted in a plateau and an uncertainty of how to correct the situation. The studies noted above suggest this is not the last plateau that will occur, though the causes and solutions may vary through time. Research is also not the only area where faculty members can plateau (though it is the most frequently cited). Teaching innovation and engagement also can be impacted.

BREAKING THROUGH THE CAREER PLATEAU

How can we help faculty members at a plateau to move to the next level? As noted in chapter 1, the first step is to help the faculty members to define a new goal. Most frequently this can be done informally, by either a senior faculty member or an administrator asking a midcareer faculty member to lunch or coffee; among the general questions about life outside of the institution and how current classes are going, a question about what new and exciting things they are doing in research can be raised. This needs to be done carefully, to avoid being misinterpreted as a reproach rather than the expression of interest and concern that it is.

If the midcareer faculty member has a plan, great; feel free to move back to the more pleasant topics such as recently read mystery novels or blockbuster movies and then just check back in occasionally. If on the other hand, there is hesitation, a confession by the senior faculty member of their own plateaus (and we have all had them—some short, some long, but there all the same) may help get the conversation going. Sometimes, just knowing they are not the only one going through the experience can help the midcareer faculty member open up and seek help.

At some institutions, this help can come in a formal setting that the midcareer faculty member may not know exists; here the concerned senior faculty member acts as a resource. For example, the University of North Carolina at Charlotte (Buch et al. 2011) recently established formal workshops for midcareer faculty members concentrating on goal setting (in their case explicitly linked to promotion to full professor) and creating career plans. Participation in the program is voluntary, and the goal is predefined, but preliminary results appear promising. Even without the resources to host these kinds of workshops, though, senior faculty members and administrators can offer midcareer faculty members some help in dealing with the plateau.

In considering how to move forward, however, we must remember that not everyone has the goal of promotion to full professor, and our first job is to figure out the midcareer faculty member's goal. In response to the shock and outrage of the last statement some readers may have, let me expand.

For some, promotion to full professor represents nothing more than an even higher service load and no other tangible rewards (i.e., at many smaller, resource-strapped institutions, it is not accompanied by a significant pay raise or change in job description). For others, the concept of promotion to full professor is so far in the future that it is not on the horizon yet. Therefore, let's look at this more generally and concentrate on the more short-term view of the current plateau with the idea that solving this issue has the potential long-term effect of keeping the midcareer faculty member active and engaged in case promotion becomes a goal in the future. Let's check in with one of Star's colleagues who is a bit further along in the process to see how this might work.

Dr. Dependable has done such a stellar job as chair, her colleagues in the department elected her to two consecutive terms. Her efficiency and reputation on getting things done has spread, and as a result, she has been asked to serve on multiple task forces and public outreach programs by the upper administration as well. The result is that five years after tenure, the book project she had planned to start right after tenure is now a distant memory. Additionally, because of some recent retirements, she has had to do several new class preparations in areas far removed from her own field of study.

Although she finds these new areas interesting and worth pursuing, the time invested here means she is barely keeping up with her own field of study. The good news is that the department never asks someone to do more than two consecutive terms as chair, so there is a light at the end of the tunnel! The bad news is she is not sure what to do next and is afraid that light at the end of the tunnel may be an oncoming train!

As she sits pondering her future one day, she gets an e-mail from a friend in another department with whom she served on a committee, Dr. Oldhand, asking if she wants to get together for coffee the next week. During the course of conversation over coffee and some delicious pastry at the local coffee house, Oldhand asks what Dependable is working on in terms of research/

creative actives. Dependable confesses she is not sure what to do. Rather than moving away from an uncomfortable conversation, Oldhand takes the bull by the horns and decides a monthly meeting over coffee and some practical advice is in order.

What should Oldhand do to help Dependable transition out of the chair's position back to the faculty and into a more productive stage in terms of research/creative activities? First and foremost, Oldhand needs to realize that Dependable is not her student and not a junior faculty member. Rather, they are colleagues and friends, and this is a very different type of relationship.

Peer coaching/mentoring, however, is an increasingly common phenomenon, and there is much literature out there to tap into (see Huston and Weaver 2008; and O'Meara et al. 2008 for in-depth discussions). These relationships can be formally structured, but at schools lacking mentoring for post-tenure faculty members, they can grow organically through relationships developed outside the department while serving on committees (yes, there is a benefit to service!). Alternatively, they develop because a senior faculty member or administrator reaches out to a midcareer faculty member. In our case study, it was a combination of the two, and here is how it works.

Two weeks later, Oldhand asks Dependable out for coffee again. Earlier in the conversation, Oldhand broaches the topic of research, asking Dependable what her dream project would be. By asking an open-ended question about goals, Dependable is free to revisit the area she specialized in prior to tenure (maybe picking up that book project again); to express interest in new areas that may have been sparked by preparing those new classes outside her research field; or even to make a shift to the scholarship of teaching in her field in a university setting.

The point is, the research goal can be highly varied and may relate back to the area of original training or, post-tenure, may involve a whole new area of enquiry. If the disadvantage of being at smaller, resource-strapped institutions is the lack of resources, the advantage is the ability to reinvent yourself in terms of research and the frequent exposure to other fields without moving to a new institution (see Aveni 2014 for a particularly eloquent memoir showing how this shift in focus can take place and the advantages it has).

Once a project, no matter how vague, is articulated, it can become a new goal to strive toward. Oldhand's role in this process is not only to spark enthusiasm and provide encouragement but also to help set up a group of faculty members with related interest to meet at set intervals (twice a month, or once a week) to talk. In the world of faculty development, this is known as peer mentoring at the group level (one-on-one peer mentoring is discussed in chapter 4 and directed toward teaching). These groups get called by different terms and can fill numerous functions; the role, in fact, can metamorphose through time. At its earliest manifestation, it can serve as a discussion group.

Over lunch, coffee, dinner, and so forth, faculty members from different departments interested in a related topic or theme can get together to discuss recent articles or books, each bringing a different perspective. Think of it as a book club for research (actually, in schools of education these are known as teaching circles and have a long history). For example, a theme of environmental policy could bring together philosophers interested in how nature is viewed, political scientists interested in recent environmental laws, communication scholars interested in the rhetoric of environment, and anthropologists interested in indigenous community rights to resources. Alternatively, a theme of medicine could bring together a biologist interested in cellular development, a chemist interested in biochemical reactions, and a clinical psychologist interested in the impact of stress on the immune system.

The topic of music can bring together specialists in sound production from the art school, physicists specializing in sound-wave analysis, and electrical engineers interested in instrumentation, as well as performance specialists. A theme of classic films can bring together actors, creative writers, historians, and photographers. The scholarship of teaching can bring together folks from education and any number of content fields. These discussion groups are the basis of a community of scholars discussed in the previous chapter that faculty members crave and help eliminate the intellectual isolation faculty members often feel in small departments. Discussing articles from different fields on a related topic with folks with entirely different backgrounds can spark new ideas and new ways of looking at research and creative activities.

Here we come to another, often unrealized, advantage of being at small resource-strapped universities. Interdisciplinary interaction is not only possible but also often a necessity. Small departments might result in disciplines being combined into a single administrative unit, and the small number of individuals in any one area forces us to break through our disciplinary silos to talk to folks with very different training and backgrounds. These interactions can occur when we serve on committees together (Anna Neumann and Aimee Terosky [2007] argue this is a major advantage of service) or because someone like Oldhand helps to form discussion groups.

At its most basic level, discussion groups act like the seminars of our graduate school days where we dissect articles in terms of themes, methods, theory, and contributions to the field. If a different member of the group chooses an article for each meeting, this both reconnects them to their own field, helping catch the group up on what is going on, and forces them to stretch their understanding of a topic by looking at it from other perspectives. These can lead to interdisciplinary research or the application of new perspectives to long-standing problems within a traditional discipline.

These groups can continue to function in this way for the entirety of their existence or can expand to include discussions of new research projects members are planning, collecting data on, or writing about. This can occur organically and subconsciously as the discussion group members talk about how to apply an idea to a current project they are working on.

Alternatively, they can change deliberately and consciously into discussion of current goals, sticky issues members run up against in a project, reading groups that provide feedback on each other's proposals, articles, or creative work, each week featuring a different member's project. This type of feedback is crucial on a number of levels: (1) nothing makes you clarify your own thinking more than having to explain it to someone else, and (2) nothing makes you expand the scope, and therefore impact, of a project more than integrating the views and critiques of someone outside the project.

Given the right mix of personalities, this transition from discussion to reading/critiquing group can happen on its own. More frequently, a prompt from someone like Oldhand to one or several members of the group is necessary. This transition or even the movement back and forth from discussion to reading/critique function is necessary to sustain the group long term. Sometimes they develop into interdisciplinary projects the members work on together, but the goal in setting these groups up and keeping them going is frequently much more modest.

The one thing that is absolutely necessary, regardless of the goal, is that they have a designated meeting time the members of the group place on their calendar. Missing a meeting is letting down your colleagues. It's like having a workout buddy: knowing someone else will be there and is counting on you to be there makes it more likely you will show up prepared to work rather than skipping your workout in favor of sitting in front of the TV stuffing your face with a bag of potato chips (maybe that is a bit over the top, but you get the picture).

LET'S SUM IT UP

So how do we relate this discussion back to our five steps emphasized in chapter 1? The first step, of course, is *defining a goal*. We have concentrated on research/creative activities in this chapter and have argued that setting new research or creative goals is one of the first steps in moving out of a career plateau. These research/creative goals can be a continuation of previous work or a movement in a different direction, and sometimes completely new areas.

The *challenges* to developing new goals frequently revolve around lack of time due to increasing service demands. The development and fleshing out of new goals require time to think, reflect, read, and reflect some more. This needs to be done in new and different ways than defining dissertation proposals/projects and research/creative activities leading to tenure. The major difference is the second major challenge: the lack of traditional mentors that are readily available to graduate students through their faculty advisors and to junior faculty members through university-sponsored mentorship programs.

Midcareer faculty members must think of mentoring in different ways, invoking peer mentoring through discussion, reading, and critiquing groups rather than relying on senior faculty members for one-on-one mentoring. The role of concerned senior faculty members and administrators is to recognize this challenge and help facilitate the bringing together of these groups. This means being aware of what midcareer faculty members outside your research areas and administrative units do. In this sense, a third challenge might lie in finding engaged senior faculty members and administrators to take these roles, as will be pointed out in later chapters.

Despite these challenges, success is possible, and this lies in the *strengths* of the midcareer faculty member's training and institutional structure. One of the positive aspects of small, resource-strapped institutions, and one of the reasons so many of us dedicate our careers to them despite the challenges, is their flexibility and willingness to break through the bounds of disciplinary silos. Due to the combining of multiple disciplines into larger administrative units, the concentration on breadth rather than depth in any one area, and the broad web of contacts made through serving on committees, individuals of very different backgrounds and foci can be integrated into peer-mentoring groups in new and unexpected ways.

A result of these diverse groups is midcareer faculty members are exposed to a mire of ideas, methods, and research/creative topics outside the scope of their original training. This strength can be tapped into as a powerful intellectual *resource*. The formation of discussion groups to keep current on the literature can spark new ideas leading to the formation and clarification of new research goals. Some of these discussion groups may fizzle and disband after a time; others will remain as long-term meetings.

The most profitable groups develop strong peer mentoring that expands their roles and morphs into settings that create and solidify *plans* of actions as reading/critiquing groups. They become safe places to brainstorm, develop research designs, and read and critique each other's articles, monographs, novels, poems, musical compositions, art, and so forth. Faculty members in education (teaching circles) and creative writing (reading groups) have used these successfully for some time. These methods of peer mentoring need to be emphasized and supported in these areas and expanded into other fields as a powerful forum for peer mentoring at the group level.

REFERENCES

Aveni, Anthony. 2014. *Class Not Dismissed: Reflections on Undergraduate Education and Teaching the Liberal Arts.* Boulder: University Press of Colorado.

Baldwin, Roger G. 1990. "Faculty Career Stages and Implications for Professional Development." In *Enhancing Faculty Careers: Strategies for Development and Renewal*, edited by Jack H. Schuster and Daniel W. Wheeler, 20–40. San Francisco: Jossey-Bass.

Baldwin, Roger, Deborah DeZure, Allyn Shaw, and Kristin Moretto. 2008. "Mapping the Terrain of Mid-Career Faculty at a Research University: Implications for Faculty and Academic Leaders." *Change* 2008 (September/October): 46–55.

Baldwin, Roger G., Christina J. Lunceford, and Kim E. Vanderlinden. 2005. "Faculty in the Middle Years: Illuminating an Overlooked Phase of Academic Life." *Review of Higher Education* 29 (1): 97–118.

Buch, Kimberly, Yvette Huet, Audrey Rorrer, and Lynn Roberson. 2011. "Removing the Barriers to Full Professor: A Mentoring Program for Associate Professors." *Change* 2011 (November/December): 38–45.

Hagedorn, Linda Serra. 2000. "Conceptualizing Faculty Job Satisfaction: Components, Theories, and Outcomes." *New Directions for Institutional Research* 105: 5–21.

Huston, Theresa, and Carol L. Weaver. 2008. "Peer Coaching: Professional Development for Experienced Faculty." *Innovative Higher Education* 33: 5–20.

Neumann, Anna, and Aimee LaPointe Terosky. 2007. "To Give and to Receive: Recently Tenured Professors' Experiences of Service in Major Research Universities." *Journal of Higher Education* 78 (3): 282–310.

O'Meara, Kerry Ann, Aimee LaPointe Terosky, and Anna Neumann. 2008. *Faculty Careers and Worklives.* ASHE Higher Education Report 34, no. 3. San Francisco: Jossey-Bass.

Strage, Amy, and Joan Merdinger. 2014. "Professional Growth and Renewal for Mid-Career Faculty." *Journal of Faculty Development* 28 (3): 41–50.

Wilson, Robin. 2012. "Why Are Associate Professors So Unhappy?" *Chronicle of Higher Education* 58 (38): A3–A4.

Chapter Four

Mentoring Senior Tenured Faculty

The "graying of the profession" has long been recognized, and several recent studies have commented on the benefits of having a mature and established faculty base to serve as mentors for junior faculty members who come into colleges and universities as the baby boomer generation retires (Huston and Weaver 2008; Lindholm et al. 2005; Schuster and Finkelstein 2006; Sorcinelli 1999; Zeig and Baldwin 2013). Mentoring programs for senior faculty members themselves, however, are extremely rare (Zeig and Baldwin 2013). You may be saying to yourself, "Well yeah, but they should have figured it out by now!" However, as is pointed out in chapter 1, *everyone* needs access to mentoring.

Of those programs that do exist for the senior faculty, it is sometimes difficult to evaluate their usefulness to other institutions because of the inconsistent definition of what constitutes senior faculty. A senior faculty member can be defined as anyone who has reached the rank of full professor regardless of age, faculty members who are older than fifty-five regardless of rank, faculty members who are one to three years from retirement, and so forth. Needless to say, the mentoring needs of a faculty member who plans to retire in one to three years and has been a teacher and researcher for more than thirty-five years are considerably different from those of someone in their midforties and newly promoted to full professor. Regardless of the definition, challenges senior faculty members face and the skill set they bring to the table are considerably different than those of a junior faculty member newly hired to the institution. Because we concentrated on research for mid-career faculty, we'll concentrate on teaching in this chapter. A case study sets the stage.

Dr. Accomplished has been at Middle States University for twenty-five years now and is still active in research and service. She is looking forward to the next ten years before she retires. She sees a decade of fulfilling work to come. She has only one concern—teaching.

She has tried to express her concerns to her colleagues in her department, but they laugh her off. After all, she has won numerous teaching awards, is always available to junior faculty members having issues ranging from university policies on curriculum to ways of motivating graduate students, and she has numerous students (undergraduate as well as graduate) working with her on projects. Given all this, what could she possibly need help with?

Recently, a memo came from the upper administration requiring departments to increase the number of classes taught online to accommodate increasing student enrollment; at the same time, two classroom buildings are being pulled from use to facilitate long-overdue upgrades to the structures and HVAC systems, and conversion of the rooms to "smart classrooms." The administration provided web training for online class preparation to help accomplish this.

The prospect of teaching online has struck fear in her very heart! After all, she usually blocks out a minimum of four hours just to figure out the new online system the bookstore uses for ordering textbooks and she curses the IT department of the university every time they update the web page or insist she upgrade to the newest version of software. She came of age in a period before personal computers, does not participate in the myriad outlets for social media, and had to get the neighbor kid to set up her new TV and DVD for her—in short, she doesn't know a tweet from a Tumblr blog and doesn't want to! How is she supposed to teach classes online when she can't figure out the software, much less translate the pedagogy?

This is made worse when the only resource she can find is on the university's web page, which she has difficulty navigating. The whole prospect is keeping her up late at night with worry, and she is trying to figure out how she can afford to take an unpaid leave of absence until the construction is over and she can return to classes where she and the students are in the same room at the same time!

Keeping up with technological change on top of all of the changes in their individual fields of study and pedagogical advances in teaching is a major undertaking for any faculty member, even when not faced with the prospect of teaching online. Unlike their younger colleagues who grew up surrounded by technology, many senior faculty members have a much more limited knowledge base to build upon, and this causes considerable anxiety. Before talking about mentoring on this issue, we begin with a more general discussion of the challenges senior faculty members face and the considerable skill sets they already possess. For the purpose of this discussion, senior faculty members are defined as individuals who are contemplating retirement in the next one to ten years.

REALITIES OF LIFE AS A SENIOR FACULTY MEMBER

Recent surveys of job satisfaction demonstrate senior faculty members tend to have higher levels of job satisfaction than junior and midcareer faculty members (Baldwin 1990; Bataille and Brown 2006; Lindholm et al. 2005; Seldin 2006; Sorcinelli 1999). They have accomplished a number of goals in terms of research, care deeply about teaching, and have provided considerable service to their departments, institutions, and profession, often taking on leadership positions for a time. The key to maintaining this positive attitude is staying engaged in all three areas of their jobs (research, teaching, and service; List and Sorcinelli 2007).

There are challenges, however, in maintaining that engagement, and some, even some highly productive senior scholars, can become disillusioned with their institutions due to a perceived lack of support in terms of mentoring as well as other areas and remove themselves from the community life of their departments. This deprives other members of the department of both their institutional knowledge and their vast well of experience in finding solutions to difficulties with research, service, and students.

At the simplest level, the growing age gap between senior faculty members and their students and sometimes the junior faculty members of their department is a challenge, and senior faculty members may find it increasingly difficult to relate and communicate with students and colleagues as they lose shared historical references and ways of communicating. Aside from the increasing use of social media by students and younger faculty members that may baffle and surprise, there are difficulties in simple conversations as references to popular culture, cultural events, and interests/hobbies outside of work diverge.

Senior faculty members are horrified to find students no longer laugh at (or even get) their jokes or understand references to daily life that they attempt in class to make the material relevant to the students' lives. This can lead to feelings of isolation, marginalization, irrelevance, and abandonment by their colleagues (Blaisdell and Cox 2004; List and Sorcinelli 2007; O'Meara, Terosky, and Neumann 2008; Seldin 2006). These feelings can be intensified if their concerns are dismissed (as in our case study) or if they mirror previous negative experiences in their careers.

Changes in administrative directives that fail to honor past successes and appear to represent the latest fad without consideration of the directive's impact on the faculty or the logistical difficulty in carrying them out can further exacerbate these feelings (Baldwin 1990; Huston, Norman, and Am-

brose 2007; Russell 2010; Sorcinelli 1999). Although frustration with changing directives is felt by everyone, resources for senior faculty members
adapting to them are particularly lacking.

In a web review of faculty development programs nationwide in the area
of teaching, Michael Zeig and Roger Baldwin (2013) found almost all resources were directed at the junior faculty despite considerable data demonstrating senior faculty needs (Bataille and Brown 2006; Gappa, Austin, and
Trice 2007; Huston and Weaver 2008). In terms of pedagogy, course mechanics, university policy, and organization of class content, senior faculty
members draw upon a wealth of experience compared to junior faculty members, resulting in questions that are considerably more nuanced and sophisti-
cated.

In terms of technology, however, they often need information that is
much more basic than do their younger colleagues who are constantly con-
nected to electronic devices and social media (Huston and Weaver 2008;
Lindholm et al. 2005). Because of the concentration on the junior faculty
noted in previous chapters, most workshops and training sessions put on by
teaching centers and mentoring relationships sponsored by centers for faculty
development are completely inappropriate for senior faculty members.

More specifically, using a one-size-fits-all approach to programs, such as
teaching online in the case study, does not provide the basic technological
information senior faculty members may need. Further, the presence of basic
modules on how to create a syllabus and engage students will likely be too
basic for these experienced teachers and leave the senior faculty members
bored and disheartened with the training at best, and insulted at being talked
down to at worse. The question "have you ever even been in front of an
Introduction to _____ [enter your field of study here] class before?" is a
frequently thought, if not spoken, complaint. Faculty development programs
and teaching consultations that do not take this into consideration reinforce
senior faculty members' feelings of isolation, and as a result, senior faculty
members may hesitate to seek help for teaching in the future (Piccinin and
Moore 2002).

Realities of Teaching for Senior Faculty

A nationwide survey of 40,670 faculty members from 421 institutions of
higher learning in 2004 clearly demonstrates the importance of teaching to
faculty. Ninety-eight percent of faculty members participating in the survey—regardless of age, rank, or institution type—stated good or excellent
teaching was a personal goal (Lindholm et al. 2005). Although they share
this goal, *how* faculty members attempt to achieve it and where they feel
themselves lacking does differ by age. In particular, senior faculty members
"report experiencing at least some stress related to keeping up with informa-

tion technology" (Lindholm et al. 2005, 20), stress that was largely lacking for the junior faculty.

Smaller studies concentrating on in-depth interviews (O'Meara, Terosky, and Neumann 2008; Russell 2010; Shih and Sorcinelli 2007; Sorcinelli 1999) indicate senior faculty members see the benefit to their students that technology offers, particularly in its facilitation of extended and thoughtful discussion sessions (a traditional seminar method of instruction previously constrained by time and space) and the ability to connect with more diverse resources. At the same time, resources to aid the senior faculty in mastering the skills needed to effectively use technology are often directed at the junior faculty or assume all faculty members have similar backgrounds and needs.

The key to creating successful mentoring programs around educational technology for the senior faculty is to remember the following: (1) they are a heterogeneous group; (2) their needs and experiences differ considerably from junior faculty; and (3) they tend to know their own needs and understand their particular learning style better than their junior colleagues to whom teaching is a new phenomenon (Blaisdell and Cox 2004; Shih and Sorcinelli 2007; Sorcinelli 1999; Zeig and Baldwin 2013).

The limited programs that do exist specifically for senior (or at least not very junior) faculty members consistently demonstrate that "hands-on" activities on the computer with a technical expert nearby should always be part of the process to increase familiarity with technology. Beyond this, three types of mentoring programs have proven to be particularly useful: mentoring up, peer mentoring, and senior faculty learning communities (SFLCs). All three of these require minimal financial resources or even time on the part of administrators interested in helping the senior faculty. Rather, in all three types of programs, they should, to paraphrase Muriel Blaisdell and Milton Cox (2004), facilitate setting up the process and then get out of the way.

Mentoring Up

One of the easiest mentoring programs for the senior faculty to engage in is "mentoring up," largely because it builds on existing relationships. Mentoring up relies on existing mentoring relationships between junior and senior faculty members to make them truly two-way streets beneficial to both parties. That is, as the senior faculty helps the junior faculty learn the culture of the institution and strategically plan research projects, where to apply for funding, where to submit papers for publication, and how to deal with disruptive students, the junior faculty can help the senior faculty with technology change. In addition to helping senior faculty members and giving them a contact for when they have a question, it shifts the relationship from a one-directional one (as junior faculty members had with their faculty mentor in graduate school) to a two-way relationship between colleagues. In other words, it helps to reduce hierarchical barriers and can strengthen the sense of community in the department.

You may be asking yourself, if it's so easy why isn't it happening spontaneously everywhere? The biggest roadblock to mentoring up is overcoming the perception of the mentor-mentee relationships by the mentor/senior faculty member. When asked, junior faculty members are usually happy to help if they have a good relationship with their mentor. Mentors frequently hesitate to ask though; they see their role as the helper and guide rather than one needing help and guidance. Sometimes they hesitate because they feel it will make them look out-of-date or unqualified, or worse, put them in the dreaded "deadwood" category, to the junior faculty. Other mentors may hesitate because they know junior faculty members can be overwhelmed as they adjust to their new positions and do not want to add a burden to their load.

How do we overcome these perceptions and make mentoring relationships a two-way street in which mentoring up is possible? The best formal mentoring programs include some training for the senior faculty volunteers. This training should be expanded to include the concept of mentoring up and how to ask for help without overwhelming the junior faculty. Likewise, junior faculty members are introduced to mentoring programs during orientation. Participation should be voluntary, and for those inquiring about the program they should be initiated with discussions about how this is different from student-teacher relationships they had in graduate school and that in the best relationships the mentoring pair learns from each other (though not the same things and frequently not the same amount).

Peer Mentoring

Peer mentoring links two individuals at similar points in their careers (in our case, two senior faculty members) in a peer relationship. In large, well-funded research universities with large departments, these partnerships can occur within a single disciplinary field and be facilitated by coteaching a class, but at small, resource-strapped institutions, where departments are small and coteaching rare, they occur across disciplines. These relationships can arise spontaneously out of connections people make on service committees.

Additionally, deans and directors of centers for faculty development can facilitate them by putting out a call for interested people to come to an organizing meeting where new connections can be made. The advantage of peer mentoring is that individuals with similar levels of teaching experience can get together to discuss problems and possible solutions. The key to success is that each member enters the relationship voluntarily and approaches the pairing with mutual respect, recognition of the considerable skill sets they each possess, and guaranteed confidentiality so that each member of the pair can freely express concerns and ask for feedback in a supportive and protected environment.

Once peer relationships are established, each member of the team decides what issue or problem they wish to concentrate on. They can be different issues or shared concerns. Sometimes these problems are solved through discussion and brainstorming. For example, Professor A might say he is frustrated that students aren't reading all of the articles assigned for a senior-level seminar class, and therefore the discussions end up superficial and he ends up lecturing on basic information instead of delving into the nuances of the issue.

Professor B may respond that she also used to have that problem until she started requiring a one-page abstract of each article be written including a synopsis of the argument, identification of underlying assumptions, details on the methodology, and the pros and cons of the study. The students can hold onto the abstracts until the end of the class so they can reference back to them (i.e., they serve as a kind of security blanket for insecure students), but they had to hand them in at the end of the class. The students recognized the benefit of the abstracts, which serve as study guides for later research projects; they completed them without too much grumbling, and the results were much better discussions.

The next semester Professor A tried this and was pleased with the result. At the same time Professor B was struggling with how to make theoretical concepts clearer in her introductory classes and was concerned with comments on student evaluations saying her lectures were boring. Professor A stated he had success connecting students with concepts by imbedding free short videos from YouTube in his PowerPoint lectures to better illustrate a point (i.e., a picture is worth a thousand words, but a video is worth ten thousand). He pulled out his laptop and showed Professor B how to search for videos, download them, and embed them in PowerPoint slides.

These types of relationships work great for brainstorming, asking for class observations and feedback, and developing specific tools. It may not help, however, if what is needed is hands-on training with educational technology that neither of the peer mentors understands. SFLCs can fill this void.

Senior Faculty Learning Communities

Senior Faculty Learning Communities (SFLCs) require the most investment by the administration to be useful. They work best when they have a specific goal or skill at their center on which all participants wish to concentrate. The SFLC meets on a set schedule (once every other week, for example), extends over a semester or academic year, and has time for structured hands-on learning, discussions, and reflection.

To get senior faculty members to participate, the administration needs to make sure they are seen as not remedial or punishment but rather respected training in which existing skills are honored and built upon. The participants can report back on their new ideas to their departments, thus spreading the word. When they are first beginning, recruitment of well-respected faculty members recognized for their teaching prowess will enhance the reputation of the program.

The SFLC should have two components at minimum. The first is technical and practical. For example, if the SFLC is built around construction of online courses (as is needed in our case study), it must have a section on the software involved to set up the class. This works best when it is a combination of an IT specialist telling the participants general principles combined with time to apply the principles to an actual class (I suggest one they have taught in a face-to-face format before) so participants can see it in action in a context they are familiar with.

The second component needs to be a participant-directed discussion session on pedagogy where brainstorming on how information needs to be presented differently online than in traditional face-to-face classes, how to spark online discussions with depth and nuance among the students, and what hands-on projects work well for students to master methodology. It is important for the faculty to lead these discussions because issues rarely center on course mechanics (syllabi, tests, and grading rubrics) that are needed by the junior faculty. Rather, they center on nuanced issues identified by experienced teachers with decades of experience.

There also needs to be time to reflect, think, and occasionally come back to a topic for a second look. One of the major differences studies have found between junior and senior faculty members participating in learning communities is the desire by senior faculty members for time to reflect and revisit new methods and techniques so they can be thoroughly vetted and considered in different contexts and applications (Blaisdell and Cox 2004; Piccinin and Moore 2002). That means the SFLC may continue for several semesters rather than being restricted to a single short workshop on new technology or the one-semester program frequently used by junior faculty. These continued meetings may deal with new issues that come up or discuss new/different solutions for old problems.

LET'S SUM IT UP

The *goals* for the senior faculty frequently tend to concentrate on the short term. That is, they generally have a specific issue, such as teaching technology, they are concerned with and already know how these short-term goals fit into the larger framework. This grasp of the "big picture" is one of the *strengths* they bring to the table, along with considerable expertise in teaching, research, and service. For example, in terms of teaching, which we have concentrated on in this chapter, they already know the types of theory and method the students generally grasp quickly and which ones they tend to have trouble with.

The *challenges* are often very specific and, in the case of teaching, related to rapidly changing technology. The *resources* include the IT staff of the university, but to be really successful, programs need to go beyond the technology and tap into junior faculty members who can mentor up and other senior faculty members at the institution who can participate in one-to-one peer mentoring. After all, the IT staff and younger faculty members of the university are fully enmeshed in the technology of today. They sometimes have great difficulty relating to senior faculty members who did not grow up with the electronic connectivity that dominates today. The *plan* needs to involve both the technology experts and the interaction with other senior faculty members with similar frames of reference to reduce the feelings of isolation and technological marginalization these faculty members frequently feel.

REFERENCES

Baldwin, Roger G. 1990. "Faculty Career Stages and Implications for Professional Development." In *Enhancing Faculty Careers: Strategies for Development and Renewal*, edited by Jack H. Schuster and Daniel W. Wheeler, 20–40. San Francisco: Jossey-Bass.

Bataille, Gretchen, and Betsy E. Brown. 2006. *Faculty Career Paths: Multiple Routes to Academic Success and Satisfaction*. Westport, CT: Praeger.

Blaisdell, Muriel L., and Milton D. Cox. 2004. "Midcareer and Senior Faculty Learning Communities: Learning throughout Faculty Careers." *New Directions for Teaching and Learning* 97: 137–48.

Gappa, Judith M., Ann E. Austin, and Andrea G. Trice. 2007. *Rethinking Faculty Work: Higher Education's Strategic Imperative*. San Francisco: Jossey-Bass.

Huston, Theresa A., Marie Norman, and Susan A. Ambrose. 2007. "Expanding the Discussion of Faculty Vitality to Include Productive but Disengaged Senior Faculty." *Journal of Higher Education* 78 (5): 493–522.

Huston, Theresa, and Carol L. Weaver. 2008. "Peer Coaching: Professional Development for Experienced Faculty." *Innovative Higher Education* 33: 5–20.

Lindholm, Jennifer A., Katalin Szelényi, Sylvia Hurtado, and William S. Korn. 2005. *The American College Teacher: National Norms for the 2004–2005 HERI Faculty Survey*. Los Angeles: Educational Research Institute, University of California.

List, Karen, and Mary Deane Sorcinelli. 2007. "Staying Alive . . ." *Journal of Faculty Development* 21 (3): 173–77.

O'Meara, Kerry Ann, Aimee LaPointe Terosky, and Anna Neumann. 2008. *Faculty Careers and Worklives*. ASHE Higher Education Report 34, no. 3. San Francisco: Jossey-Bass.

Piccinin, Sergio, and John-Patrick Moore. 2002. "The Impact of Individual Consultation on Teaching of Younger versus Older Faculty." *International Journal for Academic Development* 7 (2): 123–34.

Russell, Brendan C. 2010. "Stress in Senior Faculty Careers." *New Directions for Higher Education* 151: 61–70.

Schuster, Jack H., and Martin J. Finkelstein. 2006. *The American Faculty: The Restructuring of Academic Work and Careers*. Baltimore: Johns Hopkins University Press.

Seldin, Peter. 2006. "Tailoring Faculty Development Programs to Faculty Career Stages." *To Improve the Academy: Resources for Faculty, Instructional and Organizational Development* 24: 137–46.

Shih, Mei-Yau, and Mary Deane Sorcinelli. 2007. "Technology as a Catalyst for Senior Faculty Development." *Journal of Faculty Development* 21 (1): 23–31.

Sorcinelli, Mary Deane. 1999. "Post-Tenure Review through Post-Tenure Development: What Linking Senior Faculty and Technology Taught Us." *Innovative Higher Education* 24 (1): 61–72.

Zeig, Michael J., and Roger G. Baldwin. 2013. "Keeping the Fire Burning, Strategies to Support Senior Faculty." *To Improve the Academy: Resources for Faculty, Instructional and Organizational Development* 32: 73–88.

Chapter Five

Mentoring Non–Tenure-Track Faculty

In the last two decades there has been an explosion in the number of faculty members in non–tenure-track ranks, as well as in the number of non–tenure-track position types. These include both part-time and full-time faculty members, as well as faculty members on short-term (a semester or quarter) and long-term (decades of service) contracts, fulfilling a variety of roles.

In addition to long-established positions like artist-in-residence and research faculty members paid on grants, other titles have been expanded into new areas, and new titles have been created. For example, although the titles of clinical-teaching track and professor-of-practice have long been used for a restricted number of individuals in the professional schools, they are now found throughout the university to represent individuals who combine classroom teaching, student mentoring, and program coordination. Further, non–tenure-track teaching faculty members are known under a host of titles including lecturer, instructor, contingent faculty, and part-time faculty (even when working full-time for the institution).

By far, the area that has seen the biggest explosion of non–tenure-track faculty is the area of teaching, particularly undergraduate teaching. In terms of head count, the majority of all faculty appointments are non–tenure track in the United States (Eagan, Jaeger, and Grantham 2015; Gappa 2000; Kezar 2013; O'Meara, Terosky, and Neumann 2008; Shaker 2013; Thedwall 2006; Waltman et al. 2012). Similar patterns are found in the United Kingdom, Canada, and Australia (Nadolny and Ryan 2015).

Analysis of U.S. Department of Education data indicate "48% of faculty at doctoral and research universities and 62 percent at all U.S. degree-granting institutions are non–tenure track" (Waltman et al. 2012, 411–12; see also Shaker 2013; and Thedwall 2006). In short, non–tenure-track faculty members (both part-time and full-time) are a crucial part of the university, are increasing in number, and are likely to remain so for the foreseeable future. Unfortunately, policies and mentoring practices are frequently decades behind this new reality (Kezar 2013; Nadolny and Ryan 2015).

Most scholars (Bataille and Brown 2006; Eagan et al. 2015; Levin and Hernandez 2014; Thedwall 2006) argue the explosion of non–tenure-track teaching faculty is a reaction to the volatility and increasing unpredictability in student enrollments that can witness huge increases in one year and dramatic decreases the next. This volatility is combined with shrinking contributions to higher education from both public and private sectors and the impact of a volatile stock market on university endowments.

Because non–tenure-track teaching faculty can be hired on short-term contracts that specify enrollment targets for their classes, their use allows institutions to rapidly add or cancel classes. Additionally, because non–tenure-track faculty members are often paid considerably less than their tenure/tenure-track colleagues and, if part-time, often lack benefits, they represent substantial cost savings to the institution. Tied to this lack of investment in non–tenure-track faculty is a lack of resources at the most basic level, such as a place to meet students for office hours, or a higher-order issue such as a lack of mentoring and faculty development. A case study illustrates.

Dr. Goodguy graduated with a newly minted PhD degree in engineering from Prestigious University and faced a dilemma. His wife was recently offered a job as the head of the research and development department for a national company. His wife, their two young children, and he moved to Northwest Metropolis so she could take advantage of this opportunity.

That decision was easy; the dilemma came in what he would do next. He could attempt to find a job with one of the local industries, but he had gotten a taste of teaching during graduate school and discovered that he not only enjoyed it but also was very good at it. Therefore, he applied to the local university for a teaching job and was delighted with an offer of an 80 percent–time contract (three classes per term) for a non–tenure-track undergraduate teaching position. This gave him some flexibility to be with his young children, pass his passion for engineering on to undergraduate students, and he hoped, still be a member of a community of scholars.

We next check in with Goodguy ten years down the road. He is still teaching three classes a term; in fact, he is teaching the same introductory classes he started with. He still enjoys interacting with students and is still getting stellar student evaluation. Furthermore, his department chair fought for and got him a raise last year. Unfortunately, it was the first raise he had gotten in ten years. The lack of frequent raises is annoying but not his major source of frustration (and he certainly appreciates his chair's willingness to go to bat for him).

His frustration stems from the fact that he still does not have a permanent office, or even a desk area, at which he can meet with students, and the only way he gets an updated laptop to teach with is if he buys it himself. Even worse than this is that the permanent tenure/tenure-track faculty members never talk to him, and most do not even know his name after ten years of dedicated service to the program. This frustration is so great he now comes to campus only when he is teaching, no longer attends any events on campus, and is considering getting out of the department altogether, which would be a huge loss to the students.

What can senior faculty members and administrators do to help non–tenure-track faculty members in these types of situations? How do we make non–tenure-track faculty members feel included and valued? Given the proliferation of the types of non–tenure-track faculty members at universities today, how do we provide mentoring when the experiences and relationships are so varied and fluid? An examination of some data on the nature of non–tenure-track work will set the scene. Because teaching faculty members are, by far, the most common non–tenure-track position, I concentrate on this group here.

REALITIES OF LIFE OF NON–TENURE-TRACK FACULTY

One of the challenges in writing about non–tenure-track faculty, even those limited to teaching roles, is the variability in the nature of their appointments. Non–tenure-track teaching faculty members can be part time, paid per class and not eligible for benefits, or employed full time with benefits; they may be hired for a single semester with the possibility, but no guarantee, of renewal, or they may have multiyear contracts. They may be employed full-time outside the academy and occasionally teach a single class in their area of expertise; they may work part-time at a number of colleges and universities; or they may work full-time exclusively for a single university (Gappa 2000; Thedwall 2006).

Regardless of where they fall on these continuums, many non–tenure-track faculty members have long-term commitments to their institutions and genuinely care about the education and success of their students. Based on the results of large-scale surveys of non–tenure-track faculty members sponsored by the American Federation of Teachers and the National Center for Educational Statistics, it is clear that a large number of non–tenure-track teaching faculty members with full-time positions have held their positions for more than a decade (Gappa 2000; Levin and Hernandez 2014; Shaker 2013), and most (67.9 percent) hold terminal degrees in their fields (Levin and Hernandez 2014).

Based on the analysis of nationwide surveys (Eagan et al. 2015; Gappa 2000) and more in-depth interviews with focus groups and individual faculty members (Bataille and Brown 2006; Kezar 2013; Levin and Hernandez 2014; Shaker 2013; Waltman et al. 2012), non–tenure-track teaching faculty can be broken into two groups (voluntary and involuntary), each of which has two subgroups (part-time and full-time). Yes, you guessed it. This is the part of the chapter where I throw data at you, though I will make it as painless as possible.

The first group most studies recognize are those that choose their current position as an ideal match to their personal goals. These individuals are known as choosers or voluntary non–tenure-track faculty. Consistent results from both nationwide surveys and in-depth interviews with smaller focus groups demonstrate several consistent themes for the reasons individuals choose these positions. Most frequently cited is that the position allows them to concentrate on teaching and interaction with students (O'Meara et al. 2008) rather than being pulled away from teaching to participate in service and committee work and the stress of having to publish and constantly develop new research and creative projects required of tenure-track faculty members (Shaker 2013; Waltman et al. 2012). Those that choose part-time over full-time positions point to the flexibility these positions allow in terms of other employment as well as family (children and elderly relatives) responsibilities (Waltman et al. 2012).

The second group is involuntary non–tenure-track faculty members who aspire to either tenure-track positions or full-time employment. Many individuals who are in this position are restricted in terms of moving, usually due to spousal career concerns (Bataille and Brown 2006). Reasons given for a desire to move from non–tenure-track to tenure-track is a desire to do more research and creative work and the increased status tenure-track positions provide (Gappa 2000).

In addition to full-time faculty members who aspire to tenure-track positions are individuals who wish to stay in the non–tenure-track ranks but would prefer full-time employment with the increased wages and benefits that come with it (Bataille and Brown 2006; Gappa 2000). Occasionally, these individuals voluntarily take on administrative and advising tasks to obtain full-time status.

Based on the results of the 2010–2011 Higher Education Research Institute's survey of 4,169 non–tenure-track faculty members at 279 institutions, variability in job satisfaction is evident for these two groups. Specifically, much higher levels of work satisfaction were reported by faculty members in the voluntary group than in the involuntary group (Eagan et al. 2015). These results are supported by studies using in-depth interviews. For example, Jean Waltman and colleagues (2012) interviewed 220 non–tenure-track faculty members at twelve research universities across the United States and found that interaction with students, autonomy in the classroom, and flexibility were major sources of positive feelings for voluntary non–tenure-track faculty.

Interestingly, they also found commonalities in sources of dissatisfaction, and these dissatisfactions are shared by faculty members in both the voluntary and involuntary groups. These results are mirrored in surveys and interviews conducted by a number of researchers. Adrianna Kezar (2013) conducted interviews with 107 faculty members from twenty-five departments in three different state-supported, master's-level colleges and universities in the United States. John Levin and Virginia Hernandez's (2014) study of sixty non–tenure-track faculty members at three different institutions (a tier-one research institution, a comprehensive university, and a community college) in California was followed up with more in-depth interviews of fourteen part-time, non–tenure-track teaching faculty members from the three institutions. Andrew Nadolny and Suzanne Ryan's (2015) study is based on interviews with 130 non–tenure-track teaching faculty members in Australia.

In all four studies, institution type had little impact on the responses in terms of faculty satisfaction. Rather, department climate had the greatest impact on the faculty members' views of their position, and the impact of the department on faculty satisfaction increased considerably in departments that were seen as unsupportive of non–tenure-track faculty.

Given the consistency of the themes in these four studies and their presence in the responses of faculty members in both the voluntary and the involuntary group, the pattern appears robust and widespread. It is important to note that not everyone expressed dissatisfaction, and even when they did, they did not express dissatisfaction in all areas. However, where dissatisfaction is present, several themes appear often and across groups of different types of non–tenure-track teaching faculty, suggesting they are widespread, even among faculty members in the voluntary group. Areas of dissatisfaction fall into four areas: (1) uncertainty about teaching schedules and continued employment; (2) lack of consultation on curricular issues; (3) lack of respect from tenure-track faculty; and (4) lack of basic resources. It is important to remember that although I have separated these issues into four different themes, there is considerable overlap and they mutually reinforce each other.

One of the most frequently cited areas of frustration is over the scheduling of classes. Specifically, because non–tenure-track faculty members, especially those that are part-time, are hired as a response to wildly fluctuating enrollment numbers, classes may get added to the schedule with very little warning and thus faculty members have little time to prepare or update classes before the start of the term (Kezar 2013; Nadolny and Ryan 2015; Thedwall 2006; Waltman et al. 2012). Alternatively, non–tenure-track faculty members may have their contract terminated without warning due to either low enrollment or the need to accommodate a tenure/tenure-track faculty member's need to pick up a class because an expected grant did not material-ize or because their own class was canceled due to low enrollment. In either case, it makes employment precarious and unpredictable for the non–tenure-track teaching faculty member and is a source of stress. Even when non–tenure-track teaching faculty members have long-term contracts guaran-teeing stable employment, they may not be consulted on the best times and days for them to teach given other constraints in their lives (Kezar 2013).

The second place faculty members express dissatisfaction is with curricu-lum planning within their home department (Kezar 2013). Although they feel a considerable pride in their teaching and enjoy the autonomy of the class-room, non–tenure-track teaching faculty members are frequently excluded from discussions of pedagogy, the establishments of learning goals tied to assessment of the major, or even individual classes that may be in the cam-pus-wide core. Additionally, they are often excluded from committees plan-ning curricular updates or even from choosing textbooks (Kezar 2013) either because they are not invited or the scheduling of meetings fails to take their teaching or other obligations into consideration.

Administrators and tenure/tenure-track faculty members may fail to in-clude non–tenure-track teaching faculty members in these committees and discussions because they are trying to avoid exploiting them by requiring service not specified in their contracts or because they still view them as temporary members of the department with little to contribute to long-term curricular concerns, regardless of how long they have taught in the depart-ment. Regardless of the reason, many non–tenure-track faculty members view their exclusion as a snub and a lack of respect for their contributions and expertise because no one takes the time to explain the process or ask their opinion (Bataille and Brown 2006).

This brings us to the third theme that arose in interviews with non–tenure-track faculty members: a lack of respect shown to them by the institution in general and members of their department in particular. A frequent complaint by non–tenure-track teaching faculty members is that they feel they are treat-ed as second-class citizens (Gappa 2000; O'Meara et al. 2008). Following on our previous theme is participation in faculty governance in general and committees involved in curriculum in particular. Although many voluntary non–tenure-track faculty members cite being freed from serving on large numbers of committees as an advantage, their explicit exclusion from univer-sity service is seen as a slap in the face. Numerous interviewees stated they interpreted their exclusion as a statement by administration and the tenure/tenure-track faculty that they see the non–tenure-track faculty members as second-class citizens and that non–tenure-track faculty members are not good enough or important enough to have a voice in faculty governance (Eagan et al. 2015; Kezar 2013; Shaker 2013; Waltman et al. 2012).

Feelings that they are neither respected nor appreciated come from other sources as well. For non–tenure-track teaching faculty members with short-term contracts, there is sometimes the feeling of invisibility. For example, many institutions lack formal systems of evaluation and rarely provide feedback on performance beyond the results of student evaluations. This is especially true for term-limited faculty members who are hired on a semester-to-semester basis (Waltman et al. 2012). Because these teaching positions are tied to enrollment rather than their performance, interviewees state they feel their hard work is ignored and that contract renewal is completely divorced from how well they teach (Bataille and Brown 2006; Nadolny and Ryan 2015; Shaker 2013). Some interviewees stated that other members of the department do not even bother to learn their name or even acknowledge their presence when they are in the same room (Thedwall 2006; Waltman et al. 2012). Aside from being rude, they feel it is an explicit statement about how little they are valued as members of the department.

The lack of resources (frustration number 4) available to non–tenure-track teaching faculty members may exacerbate their feelings of invisibility and lack of respect even further. Resources fall into several areas in this discussion. First, the lack of feedback noted above is aggravated further by a lack of mentoring and faculty development for many. Aside from limited opportunities for career advancement, many institutions lack the ability to provide well-thought-out orientations to familiarize non–tenure-track faculty members on basic policies and procedures related to syllabus construction, required curriculum components for classes, and available student services for their students.

This is especially true for faculty members hired shortly before the start of the term to deal with a sudden vacancy or enrollment surges but was noted by longer-serving faculty members as well. Many departments operate on the "everyone knows that" assumption and fail to ask if they need help setting up classes, would like to view sample syllabi, or talk to others who have taught the class in the past (Kezar 2013; Nadolny and Ryan 2015; O'Meara et al. 2008; Waltman et al. 2012).

The second type of resource is on a more tangible level. Many non–tenure-track teaching faculty members are frustrated with a lack of office space to prepare class lectures, exercises, or exams as well as a place to meet with students during office hours (Eagan et al. 2015; Gappa 2000; O'Meara et al. 2008), as was seen in our case study. Another source of frustration noted by some faculty members is a lack of access to a computer (Gappa 2000; O'Meara et al. 2008), even as the integration of technology in teaching and communication with students is increasingly prevalent, and in the case of online classes required. This means that faculty members who feel the institution is not supporting them and who often earn the lowest pay in the department are increasingly expected to provide crucial aspects of the university infrastructure by providing their own computers.

So what have we learned from all of this? First, there is considerable variability among non–tenure-track teaching faculty members in terms of career goals (voluntary versus involuntary groups) and how they view their position within their department and the wider institution. Despite this diversity of goals and levels of satisfaction, there are four recurring themes that can be a source of frustration and need to be addressed. Recognizing we often have little control over enrollment trends, job security, and space for the non–tenure-track teaching faculty, there are a number of things that senior faculty members, department chairs, and deans can do to make the environment more inclusive and welcoming and to mentor faculty members in this situation.

INTEGRATING AND MENTORING NON–TENURE-TRACK TEACHING FACULTY

It is important to understand that the non–tenure-track teaching faculty is not a monolithic whole; rather, members have a variety of different goals. Although some do aspire to tenure-track positions or to move from part-time to full-time, many prefer their current position. For many in both groups, goals center on excellence in teaching and to increase their integration into their departments and access to resources to do their jobs well. Given the economic realities of higher education today, our ability to facilitate the non–tenure-track to tenure-track transition is likely limited to informing individuals of possible jobs and acting as a reference. In contrast, there are a number of things we can do to help integrate non–tenure-track teaching faculty members into our departments and to provide resources and mentoring around their teaching.

Because non–tenure-track teaching faculty members articulate most closely with their departments and their participation on committees at the institution level is limited, it is the senior faculty members in their department and, in particular, the department chair that can have the biggest impact. The feeling of invisibility and lack of feedback are two of the biggest sources of dissatisfaction. Senior faculty members and chairs can alleviate much of this with a few simple acts. Before the semester starts, send out an e-mail to the entire faculty (tenure track and non–tenure track alike) welcoming them back to campus. In that e-mail, make a point of introducing the new faculty members electronically to the rest of the department. If the department traditionally holds a beginning-of-the-year get-together/potluck or a speaker series, make sure non–tenure-track faculty members are invited. This is a small thing but has a major impact on the atmosphere non–tenure-track faculty members work in.

This general welcoming e-mail can be followed up with an e-mail to everyone teaching a class in the university-wide core or to everyone teaching a section of a class in which assessment data is collected. By reminding all faculty members of departmental and university requirements for these classes regarding syllabus policies, required learning objectives, and good assessment instruments, you provide support for all without signaling any individual out as different simply because of their contract status. This simultaneously reinforces the importance of the requirements and assessment process.

By including both the tenure-track and the non–tenure-track faculty together in the same e-mail, you are showing respect for their expertise in the classroom and removing the status distinction. Even if some classes or groups of classes are taught only by the non–tenure-track teaching faculty, there are other areas in which there is overlap. The point is, make an effort to acknowledge that the non–tenure-track faculty member's contributions in this area are of equal importance. For new faculty, a follow-up, individually directed e-mail or talk in person prior to the start of the semester is a good idea. Ask them if they need help with their syllabus or with teaching/lab supplies.

Some non–tenure-track teaching faculty members have taught elsewhere and may say thanks but no thanks, although others will welcome the gesture and treat it as an opportunity for mentoring on class mechanics. An e-mail halfway through the semester to all non–tenure-track teaching faculty members asking how their semester is going and if they need anything is often welcome. (I recommend e-mailing them separately from the tenure/tenure-track faculty for this midsemester check-in because the part-time status of many non–tenure-track teaching faculty members means the opportunity to speak to them individually is lower than for your full-time tenure/tenure-track faculty members.)

Finally, checking in at the end of the semester and thanking them for their hard work and asking them how the semester went goes a long way toward making them feel appreciated and valued. If assessment and student evaluation data come directly to the chair and results are not shared with individual faculty members by the upper administration, make sure this feedback is passed on. If the data are positive, congratulate them; if negative, set up a time to go over it and brainstorm how to improve.

The above suggestions take a minimal level of effort. Occasionally it results in a request for more guidance, in which case we strongly suggest providing it: offer to sit in on a class or to talk through how to handle a difficult student. This outreach, really just a couple of e-mails, expanding the size of your contact list for announcing speakers, and being a sounding board for problem solving, takes very little effort but does much to create a supportive and inclusive environment for your non–tenure-track faculty.

Moving from the personal touch to the structural and tangible, there are some concrete resources that can improve both job satisfaction for the non–tenure-track teaching faculty and the educational experience for the students. Office space and access to a computer is a must, even if it is shared among many part-time faculty members. In fact, Kevin Eagan and colleagues' (2015) data indicate that shared space is seen just as favorably as individual offices and computers by non–tenure-track faculty members. This is particularly true if individuals sharing the space teach on different days or at different times on the same day so that each has quiet/alone time to prepare before class or decompress after and a spot where they can talk to students without interruption.

Beyond the department level, deans can support non–tenure-track teaching faculty members as well. (I can already hear the cries of protest about limited resources and budget cuts, but let me give you two suggestions that require time rather than money, and not much time at that.) First, an orientation of a few hours for new hires can introduce the non–tenure-track teaching faculty to policies, academic calendars, and administrative issues, such as the logistics of drop/add and how to submit final grades. This investment in time up front actually saves time in the long run due to the decrease in errors that might occur otherwise.

Added on to the policies can be a short working session on setting up classes and working interactively with students in the learning management system of the university (Blackboard, E-College, CANAVS, etc.). Throw in some refreshments and time to interact more informally, and a community of teachers who serve as a network of peer mentors may arise that continues through the semester.

The second thing we recommend is establishing a teaching award that both tenure/tenure-track and non–tenure-track faculty members can apply to, or possibly several awards. For example, there may be one award for teaching lower-division classes, one for teaching upper division, and another for mentoring graduate students. No matter how you divide the awards, recognizing excellence in teaching and highlighting exceptional work in public at a reception with a certificate or plaque honors those who excel in the classroom regardless of their employment classification and demonstrates the value placed on teaching by the university. It does a great deal to remove the second-class status perception, as well providing validation of the non–tenure-track teaching faculty members' contribution to the university.

LET'S SUM IT UP

In terms of defining short-term and long-term *goals* of non–tenure-track faculty members, it is important to reach out and talk to people individually. We must get past the assumption that faculty members take non–tenure-track positions only when they have no other choice. For many (voluntary non–tenure-track faculty), it is their ideal position. For others (involuntary non–tenure-track faculty), it is less than ideal. It is important to know which group a faculty member belongs to before you can effectively help them.

Once you determine the goals, determine the strengths and challenges. The *strengths*, particularly for voluntary non–tenure-track faculty members, often lie in the dedication to their students and passion for the course material. *Challenges* are often tied to predictability of course offerings, resources, and department climate. Although many material resources and issues of predictability are out of our control, we can work to overcome these challenges with some creative scheduling and sharing of information in a timely manner. Additionally, we can provide a much more welcoming and inclusive environment for the non–tenure-track faculty to work in. The *resources* needed to accomplish this are frequently tied to a conscious effort to acknowledge the faculty members' contribution and include them within the broader departmental culture. Work with your faculty members to create a *plan* to address their concerns and work around their constraints.

REFERENCES

Bataille, Gretchen, and Betsy E. Brown. 2006. *Faculty Career Paths: Multiple Routes to Academic Success and Satisfaction.* Westport, CT: Praeger.

Eagan, M. Kevin, Jr., Audrey J. Jaeger, and Ashley Grantham. 2015. "Supporting the Academic Majority: Policies and Practices Related to Part-Time Faculty's Job Satisfaction." *Journal of Higher Education* 86 (3): 448–83.

Gappa, Judith M. 2000. "The New Faculty Majority: Somewhat Satisfied but Not Eligible for Tenure." *New Directions for Institutional Research* 105: 77–86.

Kezar, Adrianna. 2013. "Examining Non–tenure Track Faculty Perceptions of How Departmental Policies and Practices Shape Their Performance and Ability to Create Student Learning at Four-Year Institutions." *Research in Higher Education* 54: 571–98.

Levin, John S., and Virginia Montero Hernandez. 2014. "Divided Identity: Part-Time Faculty in Public Colleges and Universities." *Review of Higher Education* 37 (4): 531–57.

Nadolny, Andrew, and Suzanne Ryan. 2015. "McUniversities Revisited: A Comparison of University and McDonald's Casual Employee Experiences in Australia." *Studies in Higher Education* 40 (1): 142–57.

O'Meara, Kerry Ann, Aimee LaPointe Terosky, and Anna Neumann. 2008. *Faculty Careers and Worklives.* ASHE Higher Education Report 34, no. 3. San Francisco: Jossey-Bass.

Shaker, Genevieve. 2013. "The Road Taken: A Report on the Career Paths of a Modern Academic Workforce for Faculty Developers." *Journal of Faculty Development* 27 (3): 57–62.

Thedwall, Kate. 2006. "Nontenure-Track Faculty: Rising Numbers, Lost Opportunities." *New Directions for Higher Education* 143: 11–19.

Waltman, Jean, Inger Bergom, Carol Hollenshead, Jeanne Miller, and Louise August. 2012. "Factors Contributing to Job Satisfaction and Dissatisfaction among Non–tenure-Track Faculty." *Journal of Higher Education* 83 (3): 411–34.

Chapter Six

Advising Faculty in Hostile or Nonsupportive Departments

Separating the Perception from the Reality and the Power of Communication

There is growing concern with the issue of civility (also called faculty bullying or mobbing) between faculty members in a department. At its extreme it may require disciplinary action by the administration for particular members of the department or even placement of the department in academic receivership. If relationships in the department have reached this state, the situation is beyond the point where mentoring activities by concerned senior faculty members in other departments alone can have an impact.

There are a host of references that can help administrators dealing with departments in extreme states of dysfunction (Cheldelin and Lucas 2004; Coffman 2005; Gunsalus 2006; Higgerson and Joyce 2007; Holton 1998; Sample 2002; Stone 2009; Stone and Coussons-Read 2011; Twalle and De Luca 2008). In these situations, a concerned senior faculty member/mentor outside the department can tell the affected faculty member about resources and contacts in the office of the ombudsman or human resources. However, there often are legal implications in these situations that go beyond mentoring and require the intervention of the experts. Therefore, they are not discussed here.

Sometimes, however, the atmosphere of the department is less blatant but still viewed by the faculty as nonsupportive or hostile. These situations are sometimes hard to pinpoint and often do not rise to the level that policy and administrative action must be invoked. Rather, it takes more subtle forms. For junior faculty members, it may be the result of personality conflicts (either their own, or unknowingly walking into a long-standing dispute among senior faculty members). Alternatively, it may be the result of a conscious or subconscious attitude by the more senior members of the department that "I had to do this when I was in their position so now it's their turn." This often comes in the form of overloading individuals with service, assigning them the least popular/service classes, or a sink-or-swim approach to research mentoring.

For midcareer faculty members, it can be the result of increasing social marginalization due to long-standing personality conflicts, conflict/disagreements over the future direction of the department, or changes in directions and mission statements of the university/school/department resulting in research that is no longer in step with initiatives and funding in their academic home. Frequently, however, departments can be perceived as nonsupportive by faculty members when this is not intended.

Specifically, a less-than-collegial atmosphere can be present due to neglect, or even bad interaction or communication skills by department heads rather than active hostility. Regardless of the cause, the result is an intensification of the sense of isolation that is already present in smaller, resource-strapped units (see chapters 2 and 3) that can lead to decreased productivity, poor morale, an inability to move to the next level in the tenure and promotion process, or a drop in faculty retention. These are areas where mentoring from concerned senior faculty members can have an impact and is what we concentrate on here. Here is a case study to illustrate this point.

Dr. Integration is in his fourth year of his pretenure period in the Department of Integrated Sciences at Central Urban University (CUU). In many ways he is extremely happy at CUU. It is located in a great city, his spouse has found a wonderful job, their kids are in terrific schools, and the family loves their neighborhood and all of the activities it offers. As a result, he would really like to set down roots and stay in the area.

He also likes CUU; the resources may be constrained and the teaching commitment high, but the students are great, and ideally, the potential to break down traditional academic silos and participate in interdisciplinary research is unlimited due to the combining of multiple fields into themes rather than discipline-based departments. Heck—his department even contains a variation of his name. That has to be a good sign, right? In other words, he does not want to leave. There is only one problem: the interaction with the senior and midcareer faculty members in his department (see chapters 3 and 4 for possible causes to this).

For example, Integration is a specialist in water chemistry and has recently been talking to another junior faculty member, this one in the Department of Environmental Sciences. They share an interest in the impact of runoff from busy urban streets and parks on the health of streams running through the city. Together, they have come up with a research project that would test both biodiversity and water pollution levels in the streams and how it changes seasonally as the nature of runoff changes (fertilizer from landscaping in the summer, snow melt and road salt in the winter, and oil deposits from the road during heavy spring rains).

Even better, because the streams run right by the edge of campus, they can easily involve undergraduate students in the research project, teaching them field and laboratory methods. When the pair was discussing this one day in the break room of the Department of Environmental Sciences, the department chair, Dr. Good Communicator, wandered in for a cup of coffee. Communicator asks what has the two of them so excited and responds with enthusiasm when they lay out the program. Further, he assures them that he thinks the students will be enthusiastic and join in the data-collection process.

Excited by the stimulating conversation, Integration returns to his home department. Unfortunately, all of the office doors are closed and everyone appears to be out of the office teaching, at a meeting, or in their labs, except for the chair. Therefore, he seeks out the brand-new department chair, Dr. Overwhelmed.

Overwhelmed has received an e-mail the day before asking for a report to be written on faculty workload and class size broken down by faculty and course level. This report is due the next day, and he has no idea where to find the needed data. Just as Overwhelmed is starting to panic, a very enthusiastic Integration enters his office and starts talking about the project. At first, Overwhelmed just stares at his young colleague, having difficulty switching gears and understanding what Integration is talking about. As his narrative starts to run out of steam, Overwhelmed's only response is, "What are you talking about?"

Unfortunately, Integration, in comparing the level of enthusiasm in response between Communicator and Overwhelmed, interprets his chair's reaction as an active discouragement of the project and a devaluing of his ideas. This feeling remains even though he receives an e-mail from Overwhelmed two days later with only an FYI written in the subject line but containing an attachment about a new grant program from CUU that undergraduates can apply to for support of research projects they undertake with their faculty mentors. Because there was no statement from Overwhelmed connecting this program to their earlier conversation, Integration does not make the connection and sees it as a new and completely unrelated activity he is being ordered to undertake.

Later that week, Integration is walking across campus and stewing over the enthusiasm his colleague is receiving about the project in the Department of Environmental Sciences and what he sees as an attempt to divert him into other directions in his own department. Near the campus coffee shop he happens to run into Dr. Oldhand, the chair of the Department of Creative Arts and a friend from the library committee they both sit on. They go in for some coffee together, and after the usual pleasantries Oldhand asks, "What's new?" Integration talks about the project, the conversations with the two chairs, and the e-mail. He ends by stating how unsupported he feels and asks how he can possibly expect to gain tenure in this situation.

How should Oldhand respond? As an outside observer, she can see two possible interpretations of Overwhelmed's e-mail. The first interpretation matches Integration's. The second interpretation, which she believes more likely, is the e-mail is actually an action of support for the project by pointing out a funding source to help get the student part of the research project off the ground. How can she figure out which is the right interpretation and, if it is the latter, get Integration to change his view?

After all, she was not present at the original interactions and did not hear or experience the tone and atmosphere of the various conversations. How can she counter Integration's strongly held conviction that his department is hostile toward him and his ideas without sounding patronizing? Simply telling Integration he is wrong will add another person to his hostile list, so how should Oldhand handle this conversation? Before jumping into solutions, a little context is in order.

WHAT IS COLLEGIALITY AND WHY IS IT IMPORTANT?

A number of recent studies have dealt with the issue of collegiality (Campbell and O'Meara 2014; Coffman 2005; Keashly and Neumann 2010; Powers and Maghroori 2006; Tierney and Rhoads 1994; Trower 2012), and all note its importance in retention and morale. For example, Susan Ambrose and colleagues (2005) interviewed 123 faculty members tied to a single institution, half of whom remained at the institution and half of whom left for other universities. The issue of collegiality was "by far the single most frequently cited issue" in both groups in terms of their decisions to stay or leave the institution and their level of job satisfaction (2005, 813).

Similar results have been found in other studies (e.g., Campbell and O'Meara 2014; Trower 2012), with the department culture being paramount. For pretenure faculty, the issue of collegiality and feeling valued and supported by their department ranks particularly high. In one study, being a member of a collegial community of scholars was ranked higher than the transparency of the tenure process in terms of job satisfaction for junior faculty members (Trower 2012).

Given its acknowledged importance, you might assume we have a united definition as to what constitutes collegial behavior, but there is actually considerable variability. Some studies concentrate on the structural/procedural aspects in which there is transparency in decision making and all members of the unit work cooperatively toward collective goals (Keashly and Neumann 2010; Powers and Maghroori 2006), while others concentrate more on the nature of personal relationships in creating feelings of community and support (Tierney and Rhoads 1994; Trower 2012) or being valued for service, teaching, and research contributions (Ambrose, Huston, and Norman 2005; Campbell and O'Meara 2014).

What the studies do agree on is that one of the most important aspects of department culture and feelings of collegiality is the department chair, and this is true for faculty members at all ranks. For the junior faculty, the additional aspect of the interest expressed by the senior faculty for projects outside their own areas was of added importance (Tierney and Rhoads 1994).

In our case study, the difference in interaction and communication styles of the two department heads was paramount in Integration's interpretation of the situation. Specifically, he interpreted Communicator as more supportive and collegial than his own chair, despite the fact that Overwhelmed was the one who actually pointed him in the direction of a resource that would actually facilitate the project, not Communicator. The perception of differences in the levels of collegiality in the two departments was due to the differences in the communication style of the two chairs.

Department chairs are frequently chosen from the existing tenured faculty in the department and may rotate to a new faculty member every few years. Unfortunately, training for this administrative position is frequently nonexistent at resource-strapped institutions, and there is a steep learning curve. The result is new chairs are thrown into the position with the assumption they will figure it out eventually or they will ask for help.

For new, first-time chairs in particular, this can be a drastic and somewhat shocking transition. They are suddenly asked to shift their focus from their own research, teaching, and service activities to those of all the rest of the department. Further, they must learn all of the initiatives of the university that they have managed to ignore up to this point. Not all chairs make this transition quickly, and it frequently leads to problems. Further, early in their term, new chairs may not know all of the resources available on campus that would allow them to support their faculty's projects, and it takes a few days of investigation.

Additionally, they feel stressed and overwhelmed by the administrative responsibilities that have been added onto their already busy lives and inadvertently may send the wrong message. Junior faculty members, who are subject to their own sources of stress (as outlined in chapter 2) and feelings of isolation, may interpret the lack of time by the senior faculty members of their department in general and the department chair in particular as a lack of support (Tierney and Rhoads 1994). In one study of the impact of collegiality, junior faculty members have specifically complained that managerial and communication skills are undervalued in choosing department chairs (Ambrose et al. 2005) but do not realize that this may be due to the stress of heavy service loads and lack of training for the chair rather than a lack of caring. Further, questioning and debates about project procedures and designs are a crucial aspect of working out the details of both research and curriculum development in universities.

At all ranks, faculty members must learn to distinguish between a healthy questioning of policies/procedures and hostile personal attacks (Coffman 2005), and this is one place mentors can help. This is not always an easy thing to distinguish though, for two reasons. The first is that as academics, self-worth is often tied to our ideas, and so a questioning of an idea or a project may be misinterpreted as a questioning of intellectual capability. The second reason is that communication styles may clash, and the supportive may sound critical while the personal criticism may be masked in humor or charm.

The following quote from James Coffman encapsulates this idea.

> While the loyal curmudgeon may play a valuable role, the chronically condescending, confrontational, or threatening individual may simply be a source of stress and lost productivity for other people. The difference between the two is that the former goes after ideas, albeit in a crusty and sometimes confrontational manner; the latter goes after people, albeit in subtle and sometimes arcane ways. (2005, xv)

The manner of communication (crusty/confrontational versus subtle) may mask the actual question and motive for some individuals.

These communication problems may be magnified at schools with small programs where several disciplines are administratively cobbled together into a single department, as in our case study. In these situations, department members do not have a shared academic field as an immediate link to provide understanding. When Overwhelmed asks, "What are you talking about?" it could be the situation of a bench scientist in physics asking Integration to explain the field portion of the project and how it would be operationalized, rather than an expression of doubt. In these situations faculty members have to work at not only finding both commonalities to hold the departments together but also understanding the norms of research process and communication about it.

For junior faculty members who will be awarded on the quality and quantity of their research publications as well as the quality and innovation of their teaching, this may be particularly stressful, and negative meaning may be assigned more quickly to questions. In these situations, junior faculty members may feel they are continually justifying common situations in their field such as their choice of where to publish research or display creative works and the relative merits of single authored versus coauthored works (Keashly and Neumann 2010) to folks with a completely different paradigm of how research works. Given all this, what can Oldhand do to help the situation Integration has found himself in?

SOLUTIONS

Oldhand sees two issues she would like to address. The first is the obvious stress new chairs like Overwhelmed are feeling. She makes a mental note to herself both to check in with Overwhelmed, one chair to another, about how things are going and perhaps to offer some tips about managing the mound of paperwork involved in being a chair. Beyond this, she plans to renew her conversation with the administration of the university about the possibility of creating a chair's handbook to point chairs in the correct direction for resources they need to succeed in their new administrative responsibilities, including a master calendar so they know when major reports are due and where to collect information they need, thus reducing some of the stress and confusion involved. Ideally, the handbook would be accompanied by a series of short workshops, a monthly coffee group to discuss issues, or a pairing of new chairs with those who have some experience in an administrative mentoring system.

The second, more immediate issue, however, is Integration. Oldhand should start by talking to Integration about his water-pollution project. He is obviously excited about the collaboration, and the strengths of the proposed plan are manifold. First, it is an interdisciplinary plan with considerable importance to CUU, the city, and the field more broadly. Second, it has the potential to lead to a number of scholarly articles. Third, it will form the basis of an important and innovative experiential learning opportunity for the students. Finally, it potentially provides a service to the community and can raise the visibility of CUU in the area.

The challenges in kicking off the project are twofold. The first is time and money to support the project. Despite what Integration has assumed, this is actually the easier of the two challenges to address and is the short-term issue. The second, long-term issue is helping Integration to deal with what he perceives as a hostile and nonsupportive chair.

Telling Integration to just go talk to his chair about the issue is likely to be of little help by itself. Rather, Oldhand needs to talk to Integration about how to go about doing this. In other words, Oldhand needs to move the long-term issue to the forefront in the discussion. She can use the current project to help do this. Solving the immediate problem of how to get the project off the ground can be used to help Integration develop a communication skill set that will help him better understand the other members of his department and thus achieve long-term success at CUU.

The first step in dealing with the long-term communication issue is to find out if Overwhelmed is, in fact, hostile to the proposed project as Integration assumes or not. It is difficult to do this without further information. On the surface, it appears to Oldhand that Integration caught his chair at a bad moment and the immediate reaction had nothing to do with the project. Individual faculty members are frequently so focused on their own activities that they do not always see or even think about the stresses other members of their department are undergoing.

Add to this, senior and midcareer faculty members are often moved into administrative positions with a training program designed around the idea of throwing them into the deep end of the pool and watching to see who sinks and who swims. If you have never attempted an administrative job, you often do not know what is involved and may not see the stress others are under. A new chair may not have even thought that much about how the university outside their department operates or in some cases what others in their department do, and even less how to help them accomplish their goals.

New chairs can become overwhelmed as they are suddenly forced out of a job they have been trained for that concentrates on individual success and contributions to research, teaching, and service and are told to switch their perspective overnight to one in which the collective and the success of others is paramount. That is a huge shift in the way you view your professional world, and new chairs do not always make the transition seamlessly. They have to learn not only new responsibilities but often new ways to communicate as well.

Simply pointing all this out to Integration may mitigate his feelings toward his chair, but it is unlikely to do away with all the fears. After all, a certain level of doubt and paranoia is part of the job description for most pretenure faculty. To keep Integration from freezing up and abandoning the project out of fear, a plan of action is needed. While drinking their coffee, Oldhand should point out that chairs are responsible for a number of reports right now but that things will calm down next week. That would be an excellent time to broach the subject with Overwhelmed again. She should encourage Integration to send his chair an e-mail asking for a meeting the next week to discuss his plans for the upcoming year rather than just dropping in.

This approach allows both sides to prepare for the meeting rather than catching one or the other off guard at a bad time. If Overwhelmed was just living up to his name (i.e., he was overwhelmed) during their last encounter, this gives him a chance to finish the reports and take a breath before moving into a mentoring role for his junior faculty. In an ideal world, Overwhelmed will respond, "Yes, I would like to talk to you some more about that exciting new project you mentioned. In addition to the grant program for the student research I e-mailed you about, I've had some thoughts about how we might approach the city for some funding—let's talk!"

A response like this would immediately alleviate Integration's fears. However, if Overwhelmed has a history of communication miscues with his faculty, the e-mail may be more along the lines of, "Sure, I'm free on Wednesday at noon." If this is the response, you don't know if Overwhelmed thinks the project is a great idea and he just isn't expressing himself well or if he thinks the project is a terrible idea that will destroy his junior faculty member's chance of getting tenure. Because of the communication problem, you don't know which of these two possibilities is reality.

In counseling Integration on how to communicate with his chair at this meeting, Oldhand should help him think through some opening questions to broach the topic and figure out where Overwhelmed stands. In other words, she is mentoring Integration in effective communication. If the department has clear tenure criteria, referencing those criteria and how this new project fits them is a great place for Integration to start the conversation. Unfortunately, those are not always present. If the value of interdisciplinary research is unclear, beginning the discussion of the more traditional journals in which Integration was planning on publishing the results of the water chemistry portion of the project is a good starting point. Integration could then segue into asking about how his department ranks more nontraditional or interdisciplinary journals and funding sources or how the department evaluates applied research.

By demonstrating he is thinking of multiple publication outlets and funding sources, Integration may get clarification on Oldhand's thinking. Does the department, despite its name, maintain a more traditional stance emphasizing historical disciplinary silos and publication venues, or does it actually value interdisciplinary research more. If it is the former and he is still committed to the new project, Oldhand can help Integration think about how to construct the new project to ensure there is ample data for more traditional journals while also training the students more broadly and contributing to an interdisciplinary undertaking. If it is the latter, the department can help him think about how to integrate both traditional and nontraditional ways of going about the research.

Regardless of the research outcome, Oldhand is helping him gain an important communication skill that is just as important as his presentation of ideas. Oldhand is teaching Integration how to listen and interpret both the words and the actions of others. Oldhand needs to make sure she follows up with Integration at the end of the next week and, in particular, to ask how the meeting went. Integration may not think to report back, so Oldhand should e-mail about the meeting if she is to continue helping him.

LET'S SUM IT UP

Each chapter in this book ends with a section that pulls us back to the five steps that are important for all mentoring activities outlined in chapter 1. In this instance, Integration is very focused on the goal of his interdisciplinary project. Oldhand rightfully sees, however, that the research project is actually a short-term goal. The more important, long-term *goal* is actually learning the communication skills Integration will need throughout his career at CUU. These communication skills involve not only clearly articulating his own plans but also, just as importantly, figuring out what other people are saying.

Integration's first interpretation of the situation was that the chair of the Department of Environmental Sciences was highly supportive of the project while his own chair was not. This perception continued despite the fact that Communicator did not actually point the pair toward any resources that would help them achieve their goal while his own chair did. Learning to communicate effectively must include improvements in not only what we say (something Overwhelmed needs to work on) but also how we listen to the words and actions of others (something Integration needs to work on).

In helping achieve the long-term goal, Oldhand needs to tread carefully to both understand the relationship and offer the correct advice. If Oldhand is reading the situation correctly, the *strength* of the two parties involved is actually the same: the enthusiasm for interdisciplinary work and a willingness to try the conversation a second time.

The *challenge* is that the two parties have very different communication styles, and these styles are actually somewhat, though not impossible, to change. One of the biggest stumbling blocks is that communication style is not something most of us think about unless we specialize in the fields of communication or rhetoric. For the rest of us, it does not generally come to the fore of our thinking unless a situation blows up in our face. As such, communication issues often go unrecognized and unresolved.

To start, the primary *resource* for both Integration and his chair is Oldhand. If she is correct in her assessment of the situation, both Integration and Overwhelmed want the same thing and her job is to serve as a reality check for Integration and help him see that. The help she can provide to Overwhelmed is more subtle and behind the scenes. It is tied to the idea of the resource handbook, workshops, and mentoring for chairs. If she is wrong in her assessment, there is a bigger issue that may require a reference of the parties to the university's ombudsman. First, however, she needs to help Integration figure out what the situation is. The *plan* for this stage of the process is the meeting and the opening questions she helped Integration craft to determine the department's position.

REFERENCES

Ambrose, Susan, Therese Huston, and Marie Norman. 2005. "A Qualitative Method for Assessing Faculty Satisfaction." *Research in Higher Education* 46 (7): 803–30.

Campbell, Corbin M., and Kerry Ann O'Meara. 2014. "Faculty Agency: Departmental Contexts that Matter in Faculty Careers." *Research in Higher Education* 55: 49–74.

Cheldelin, Sandra I., and Ann F. Lucas. 2004. *Academic Administrator's Guide to Conflict Resolution.* San Francisco: Jossey-Bass.

Coffman, James R. 2005. *Work and Peace in Academe: Leveraging Time, Money and Intellectual Energy through Managing Conflict.* Bolton: Anker.

Gunsalus, C. I. 2006. *The College Administrator's Survival Guide.* Cambridge, MA: Harvard University Press.

Higgerson, Mary Lou, and Teddi A. Joyce. 2007. *Effective Leadership Communication: A Guide for Department Chairs and Deans for Managing Difficult Situations and People.* Bolton, MA: Anker.

Holton, Susan A., ed. 1998. *Mending the Cracks in the Ivory Tower: Strategies for Conflict Management in Higher Education.* Sterling, VA: Stylus.

Keashly, Loraleigh, and Joel H. Neumann. 2010. "Faculty Experiences with Bullying in Higher Education." *Higher Education, Administrative Theory and Praxis* 32 (1): 48–70.

Powers, Charles, and Ray Maghroori. 2006. "How to Avoid Having Dysfunctional Departments on Your Campus." *Academic Leader* 22 (2): 4–6.

Sample, Steven B. 2002. *The Contrarian's Guide to Leadership.* San Francisco: Jossey-Bass.

Stone, Tammy. 2009. "Departments in Academic Receivership: Possible Causes and Solutions." *Innovative Higher Education* 33: 299–38.

Stone, Tammy, and Mary Coussons-Read. 2011. *Leading from the Middle: A Case-Study Approach to Academic Leadership for Associate Deans.* Lanham, MD: Rowman & Littlefield.

Tierney, William G., and Robert A. Rhoads. 1994. *Enhancing Promotion, Tenure and Beyond: Faculty Socialization as a Cultural Process.* ASHE-ERIC Education Report 6. Washington, DC: George Washington University Press.

Trower, Cathy Ann. 2012. *Success on the Tenure Track: Five Keys to Faculty Job Satisfaction.* Baltimore: Johns Hopkins University Press.

Twalle, Darla, and Barbara M. De Luca. 2008. *Faculty Incivility: The Rise of the Academic Bully Culture and What to Do about It.* San Francisco: Jossey-Bass.

Chapter Seven

Dealing with Bias

Subtle and Not-So-Subtle Obstacles for Women and Faculty of Color

In addition to issues faced by all faculties, there are groups of faculty members who face additional obstacles and may need additional or different types of mentoring—specifically, individuals society places in the category of "other" and who, as a result, experience bias from the community, students, fellow faculty members, and the broader profession. The placement of individuals in the role of "other" is often due to issues like disabilities, sexual orientation, and religion, or because they are faculty members of color or women, especially women in STEM (science, technology, engineering, and mathematics) fields.

Because most of the research in higher education administration has been done on bias directed toward faculty members of color (particularly black/ African American) and women, this book concentrates on these two groups here, but we must all remember that bias and discrimination against other groups is just as real. Just as in chapter 6, the book does not address the type of discrimination that rises to the level of federal, state, or local law in terms of discrimination and sexual harassment/assault. If you are made aware of this type of situation, contact the appropriate authorities immediately—no ifs, ands, or buts.

Additionally, if your campus does not have policies in place regarding harassment, bullying, and discrimination, it is the ethical responsibility of senior faculty members and administrators to work to establish these (Griffin et al. 2011). Rather, we concentrate here on the issues and bias that faculty members of color and women face every day that may not rise to the level of policy/legal violation but negatively impacts their lives all the same. A case study sets the stage.

Dr. Old Hand walked into the break room to heat up his lunch and found Dr. New-Math Star sitting at the table staring in disbelief at the student evaluations from the Introduction to Applied Statistics class she taught last semester. When Dr. Hand asks what is wrong, Dr. Star's initial reaction is, "The students hate me." Because Star had been so enthusiastic about the class last semester and went above and beyond the call of duty to set up extra tutoring sessions to work with students who were struggling, Hand finds this hard to believe.

When he asks to see the summary sheet he notices that most of the students actually gave very favorable scores but a handful scored her very low. When he pointed out that most students scored her very high, Star points to the written comments. In amongst all of the appreciable comments on the extra tutoring and what a great teacher she is, there were others with comments that were very critical but center exclusively on her personal appearance and statements questioning or dismissing her knowledge of the field altogether. These were the comments Star had fixated on.

In thinking back to the previous semester, Hand remembered Star asking how to address a handful of male students in the class who insisted on calling her Miss Star instead of Doctor or Professor and demanding she provide the mathematical proof for every statistical test she introduced to the class despite the fact it was a class in application rather than derivation or statistical theory. Together, they came up with a response of, "This is an applied class, but I'm glad to see you so interested. Let's go over that after class."

The students demanding the proofs never took her up on the offer, but it did work to get the class back on track. Hand wondered if these were the same students who filled out the evaluations that distressed Star and that it was a reflection of the students not being willing to accept the expertise of a woman in what they thought of as a traditionally male field rather than a reflection of the quality of Star's teaching.

How should Hand respond? Simply telling her to ignore them is unlikely to relieve Star's anxiety or to help her deal with similar issues that might arise in the future. Before we can talk about strategies to help Star, a little context is important.

DEFINING THE STATE OF AFFAIRS AND THE TERMS

Faculty members of color and women continue to be underrepresented as faculty members in the tenure/tenure-track faculty ranks even as these groups grow in the nation's citizenry (for faculty members of color) and university student population (for both groups). Data collected by the National Center for Educational Statistics indicate only 18 percent of faculty members (combined full- and part-time; tenure/tenure track and non–tenure track) were ethnic/racial minorities, and only 6 percent were black/African American (Eagan and Garvey 2015; Griffin et al. 2011; Harris et al. 2017; Victorino, Nylund-Gibson, and Conley 2013).

Women represent 47 percent of the faculty (combined full- and part-time; tenure/tenure track and non–tenure track), but in the STEM fields it is considerably lower. For example, in engineering, only 11.8 percent of the tenure/tenure-track faculty members are women (Ward 2008). Faculty members in both of these groups are faced with hostile environments in their daily work. In a survey of 65,124 faculty members at 426 degree-granting institutions, hostile environments were noted as an area of concern for all faculty members but were felt particularly strongly by faculty members of color (especially black/African American and Latina/o faculty) and women (Victorino et al. 2013; see also Jayakumar et al. 2009). In-depth interviews with faculty members bring to light how this hostility plays out in their daily lives (Griffin et al. 2011; Harris et al. 2017). The result is increased stress and job dissatisfaction as well as increased feelings of marginalization and isolation (Eagan and Garvey 2015; Griffin et al. 2011; Jayakumar et al. 2009).

In addition to overt hostility directed toward faculty members of color and women are unconscious biases that result in the quality of their work and knowledge being challenged both in the classroom and with regard to their scholarship. For example, women are often addressed as Miss or Mrs. by their students rather than as Doctor or Professor as their male colleagues are addressed (McKendall 2000). The situation is often worse in STEM fields as women break the image of not only male professor but also male scientist—and women of color break the image even further.

A recent study shows that when students in physics are asked to evaluate the teaching skills and knowledge of physics by male and female instructors using identical scripts in taped lectures they consistently rated the women lower (Graves, Hoshino-Browne, and Lui 2017). Similarly, when students were given identical CVs where only the name was altered, CVs with African-sounding names were consistently rated lower than CVs with European-sounding names, regardless of the field of study (Bavishi, Madera, and Hebl 2010).

Lotte Bailyn (2003) found similar results when identical CVs were given to subjects to rate with the only alteration being the gender of the name; CVs with women's names were consistently rated lower (see also Handelsman et al. 2005). These biases are not restricted to the United States. In a study in Europe, the scientific accomplishments of men were consistently rated higher than those of women regardless of the gender of the rater. To achieve a similar competency score, women needed to exceed the scientific productivity of their male counterparts by sixty-four impact points (Wennerås and Wold 1997). In interviews, women and faculty members of color in the United States indicate they feel their research, teaching, and service contributions are frequently overlooked or even trivialized by their colleagues (Eagan and Garvey 2015; Handelsman et al. 2005; Harris et al. 2017; McKendall 2000; Samble 2006; Victorino et al. 2013).

When discussing discrimination and bias resulting in chilly or hostile environments, many researchers make a distinction between macro- and microaggression/bias, though Michelle Harris and colleagues (2017, 93) rightly point out that "no aggression is micro" for the person that is subjected to it. One of the reasons the distinction continues to be made, however, is that the source of the aggression/bias differs (though they are related), and therefore how we help faculty members subject to them differs.

Macroaggression is situated at the group level and is embedded within structural and institutional customs and cultures tied to historical legacies of racism and sexism. Although most universities strive to address macroaggression through policies on discrimination, sexual harassment, and bullying, much remains to be done. Additionally, depending on the social and political climate of the nation or community, instances of macroaggression can escalate periodically, both on campus and in the surrounding community. Occasionally, these escalations can erupt into violence. The increased hostility and sometimes violence that accompanies this social escalation affects faculty members both on and off campus. Senior faculty members and administrators have an ethical responsibility to implement safeguards and policies to ensure the safety of affected faculty members and to ensure our colleagues feel safe and valued.

Microaggression is situated at the personal level and is most frequently reported in the form of hostility and ridicule. This hostility comes in the form of more frequent challenges from students (Harris et al. 2017; Thompson 2006) and in the belief that they are seen by their colleagues as black/African American, Latino/a, or by their gender first and as a professional and colleague second (Eagan and Garvey 2015; Graves et al. 2017; Griffin et al. 2011; Handelsman et al. 2005).

Microaggression can manifest itself in the form of slights, ridicule, refusing to be acknowledged for ideas and service, and being ignored at meetings. One of the most pervasive consequences of microaggression is an increased feeling of isolation and marginalization. That is, the problem felt by many in resource-poor institutions and discussed in the previous chapters is magnified manifold for faculty members subject to these types of aggressive behaviors.

Additionally, because faculty members of color and women in general and in the STEM fields in particular are so underrepresented, they may find themselves in greater demand for committee work, advising, and community outreach than their white male colleagues. Studies are somewhat contradictory on the issue of standard university committee work with some studies showing high committee demands on faculty members of color and women to ensure diverse perspectives at some institutions (Eagan and Garvey 2015; Griffin et al. 2011; McKendall 2000; Thompson 2006; Ward 2008), but data from other institutions show approximately equal commitments (Porter 2007). The studies are unanimous, however, in demonstrating higher advising loads, particularly advising and career advice for students of color and women in undergraduate programs.

A number of studies that demonstrate that faculty members of color and women not only are facing increased stress, pressure, and marginalization but also are frequently cut off from informal mentoring networks, particularly with senior faculty. In terms of women, these relationships appear to be curtailed due to men's fears of rumors and innuendo regarding sexual activity (Chesler and Chesler 2002; Clark and Corcoran 1986; Winkler 2000). The result is they miss out on the socialization to their department and their feelings of isolation, marginalization, and invisibility are heightened (Cullen and Luna 1993; Darwin and Palmer 2009; Handelsman et al. 2005; McKendall 2000; Sellers, Howard, and Barcic 2008).

Recent surveys indicate faculty members of color face a similar lack of informal mentoring (Rice, Sorcinelli, and Austin 2000) that often occurs in social settings outside of work. A survey of 6,882 faculty members from eight institutions (Ponjuan, Conley, and Trower 2011) demonstrates high levels of dissatisfaction by women and faculty members of color regarding interaction with their senior colleagues. In this same survey, women tend to feel less isolated with their male peers, but faculty members of color state the same level of dissatisfaction with their white peers as with senior faculty.

The lack of access to informal mentoring relationships means faculty members of color and women often miss out on the socialization regarding the unwritten rules of departmental culture (Winkler 2000) as well as potential collaborators and material resources. This isolation and marginalization leads to feelings of invisibility and the belief that their voices are not heard on issues affecting their department and in terms of their own research accomplishments (Chesler and Chesler 2002; Cullen and Luna 1993; Griffin et al. 2011; Thompson 2006; Victorino et al. 2013). Given all this, how can concerned senior faculty members like Dr. Hand help their colleagues at all levels/ranks who face these issues?

FINDING SOLUTIONS

In large departments, faculty members can often find an individual to discuss these types of issues with, even when some in their department shy away from engaging in informal mentoring with them. In very small departments characteristic of resource-poor institutions, faculty members of color and women may not have another individual to fall back on and, therefore, become marginalized within their own departments. When this happens, concerned senior faculty members from other programs should make a more concerted effort to reach out across disciplines to discuss the unwritten rules that allow faculty members to successfully negotiate the system. For example, in addition to the usual "How are things going?" a question like "What are you doing for service and advising these days?" provides the prompt that elicits specific information on whether the faculty member is overcommitted in the area of service.

In formal mentoring relationships, faculty members learn university service expectations with regard to tenure, promotion, and yearly evaluations. It is in the informal mentoring relationships that discussions about how to say no, budgeting time, and matching service activities to research and teaching interests occurs. These issues are more complicated than they sound at first glance, and if faculty members lack informal mentoring, they may misjudge how to balance these demands, leading to serious consequences. For example, if you just say no when people ask you to do service, you may be labeled as noncollegial or not pulling your weight, regardless of how many other things you are doing, and this can increase your isolation.

In other words, impression management (one of those subtle things they never teach you in graduate school) becomes important. Informal mentoring is where we learn to change "no" to "thank you for thinking of me, but I am so overcommitted with my other service obligations I wouldn't be able to devote the time such an important project deserves. I wish you luck in finding someone for this important role."

It is also through informal mentoring that we learn to estimate the time commitment needed for each committee and the goals of the committee. If we don't learn this specifically for every committee, we at least learn the questions to ask to find this out. As senior faculty members, asking the question "What kinds of service and advising activities are you doing?" is our way of figuring out if the faculty member has been clued in on the issues of budgeting time, how to say no, and integrating service commitments with research and teaching interests. If the response is a long list of committees that are seemingly unconnected, steering the conversation toward time management and saying no is needed. If the response is that they are getting lots of requests but haven't committed yet, a discussion on the goals of the committees and the faculty member's interests is in order. If the response demonstrates the faculty member is balancing service well, move on to other topics, such as good books, recent movie releases, or that new restaurant in town.

Strategic thinking and time management is also important in terms of research. Informal research mentoring on issues other than method and theory of the field goes beyond asking for publication counts to thinking about research and its dissemination as an integrated whole. For example, attending national academic conferences is often important for establishing and maintaining professional networks, but at resource-poor institutions travel money is frequently available only if you are presenting a paper. As a result, there is a tendency to put together papers without thinking about what will happen with them once the meeting is done.

Senior faculty members should shift the question from the general "What project are you working on?" to "To what venue were you thinking of submitting your expanded conference paper?" It's important to talk to the faculty member about the balance of national/high-impact and regional/lower-impact journals and the appropriate journals for different projects. If a conference paper is a preliminary look at a project that needs more data collection, is there a cadre of students (perhaps a student club or reading group) that the faculty member could simultaneously advise and involve in the research/data-collection process? This action combines service, mentoring of students, and research interest.

Alternatively, are there faculty members in other departments that could serve as collaborators if this is missing in the faculty member's home department? Sometimes, the net should be cast even wider in terms of collaborations and networks. As a mentor you may suggest the development of expanded cross-disciplinary networks by joining associations like the Society for Chicanos/Hispanics and Native Americans in Science (SACNAS), the Association for Women in Science (AWIS), the Association of Women Engineers, Management Faculty of Color Association (MFCA), and the Black Doctoral Network.

In addition to helping faculty members balance service, teaching, and research demands, mentors can help in other areas. The studies discussed above note faculty members of color and women frequently state feelings of invisibility and a lack of acknowledgment of research accomplishments. Tell faculty members about awards in their division, at the university level, and in their discipline for service, teaching, and research. When appropriate, nominate them yourself; it's fine to act as an advocate as well as a mentor. Many faculty members are not aware of these awards, so point them out. It brings visibility and validation to faculty members and strengthens their dossiers as they go for tenure or promotion to full professor.

Finally, faculty members might just need safe locations and people to vent to, to discuss situations with, to get some perspective, and to problem solve. Dr. Star in the case study at the beginning of the chapter is in this position. Earlier in the semester she worked with Dr. Hand to come up with a response to the constant challenges by the male students in the class. In the particular instance in the break room featured in the case study, Hand could help her dissect the student evaluation to determine that most of the comments and scores were in fact favorable and to put the small handful of negative comments in perspective. Hand also should help her to develop a network of faculty members in her own and in other departments who might face similar issues—in this case women in STEM fields (Harris et al. 2017; Sedivy-Benton et al. 2014). This network can serve as a support system and help her with reality checks to sort out bullying versus constructive criticism and make a decision about how to address them.

LET'S SUM IT UP

As with the previous chapters in this volume, it is important to sum up the discussion and focus it back on the five steps put forward in chapter 1. In the case of faculty members who are facing conscious and unconscious bias, the *goal* of our mentoring activities centers on helping them find solutions to their immediate problem (such as student challenges/disruptions in class) and developing networks and strategies to help them succeed and feel safe, valued, and as integral members of the university community long-term.

Their *strengths* center on their own considerable talents and the networks of people willing to help them navigate the challenges that arise in their careers. The *challenges* are numerous and are rooted in historical contexts of racism and sexism resulting in micro- and macroaggressions/biases directed at them. The consequences of these biases can be a lack of informal mentoring; an undervaluation of their teaching, research, and service; and a sense of invisibility. In other words, that network of people noted as a strength is not always obvious to the faculty members facing these issues, and we, as concerned senior faculty members, need to help them find it.

The *resources* that can help faculty members facing these issues are dispersed and at times difficult to identify in the absence of informal mentoring. It is the job of senior faculty members to help them do this, be it providing opportunities to vent, learning the unwritten rules of the unit, interpreting the situation, finding solutions, forming a network, or promoting their work through awards and recognition. Once the nature of the problem is identified (and this may take some deeper probing than usual) and the resource that is needed is found, help the faculty member to make a *plan* to tap into these resources now and in the future.

REFERENCES

Bailyn, Lotte. 2003. "Academic Careers and Gender Equity: Lessons Learned from MIT." *Gender, Work and Organization* 10 (2): 137–53.

Bavishi, Anish, Juan M. Madera, and Mitchel R. Hebl. 2010. "The Effect of Professor Ethnicity and Gender on Student Evaluations: Judged before Met." *Journal of Diversity in Higher Education* 3 (4): 245–56.

Chesler, Naomi C., and Mark A. Chesler. 2002. "Gender-Informed Mentoring Strategies for Women Engineering Scholars: On Establishing a Caring Community." *Journal of Engineering Education* 91: 49–55.

Clark, Shirley M., and Mary Corcoran. 1986. "Perspectives on the Professional Socialization of Women Faculty: A Case of Accumulative Disadvantage?" *Journal of Higher Education* 57 (1): 20–43.

Cullen, Deborah L., and Gaye Luna. 1993. "Women Mentoring in Academe: Addressing the Gender Gap in Higher Education." *Gender and Education* 5: 125–38.

Darwin, Ann, and Edward Palmer. 2009. "Mentoring Circles in Higher Education." *Higher Education and Research Development* 28 (2): 125–36.

Eagan, M., Kevin Jr., and Jason C. Garvey. 2015. "Stressing Out: Connecting Race, Gender, and Stress with Faculty Productivity." *Journal of Higher Education* 86: 923–54.

Graves, Amy L., Etsuko Hoshino-Browne, and Kristine P. H. Lui. 2017. "Swimming against the Tide: Gender Bias in the Physics Classroom." *Journal of Women and Minorities in Science and Engineering* 23: 15–36.

Griffin, Kimberly A., Meghan J. Pifer, Jordan R. Humphrey, and Ashley M. Hazelwood. 2011. "(Re)Defining Departure: Exploring Black Professors' Experiences with and Responses to Racism and Racial Climate." *American Journal of Education* 117: 495–526.

Handelsman, Jo, Nancy Cantor, Molly Carnes, Denice Denton, Eve Fine, Barbara Grosz, Virginia Hinshaw, Cora Marrett, Sue Rosser, Donna Shalala, and Jennifer Sheridan. 2005. "More Women in Science." *Science* 309: 1190–91.

Harris, Michelle, Sherrill L. Sellers, Orly Clerge, and Fredrick W. Gooding Jr. 2017. *Stories from the Front of the Room: How Higher Education Faculty of Color Overcome Challenges and Thrive in the Academy.* Lanham, MD: Rowman & Littlefield.

Jayakumar, Uma M., Tyrone C. Howard, Walter R. Allen, and June C. Han. 2009. "Racial Privilege in the Professoriate: An Exploration of Campus Climate, Retention, and Satisfaction." *Journal of Higher Education* 80: 538–63.

McKendall, Sherron Benson. 2000. "The Woman Engineering Academic: An Investigation of Departmental and Institutional Environments." *Equity and Excellence in Education* 33: 26–35.

Ponjuan, Luis, Valerie Martin Conley, and Cathy Trower. 2011. "Career Stage Differences in Pre-Tenure Track Faculty Perceptions of Professional and Personal Relationships with Colleagues." *Journal of Higher Education* 82 (3): 319–46.

Porter, Stephen R. 2007. "A Closer Look at Faculty Service: What Affects Participation in Communities." *Journal of Higher Education* 78 (5): 523–41.

Rice, R. Eugene, Mary Deane Sorcinelli, and Ann E. Austin. 2000. *Heeding New Voices: Academic Careers for a New Generation.* Washington, DC: American Association for Higher Education.

Samble, Jennifer N. 2006. "Female Faculty: Challenges and Choices in the United States and Beyond." *New Directions for Higher Education* 143: 55–62.

Sedivy-Benton, Amy, Gabriele Strohschen, Nora Cavazos, and Carrie Boden-McGill. 2014. "Good Ol' Boys, Mean Girls, and Tyrants: A Phenomenological Study of the Lived Experiences and Survival Strategies of Bullied Women Adult Educators." *Adult Learning* 26 (1): 35–41.

Sellers, Darlene F., Valerie M. Howard, and Maureen A. Barcic. 2008. "Faculty Mentoring Programs: Reenvisioning Rather than Reinventing the Wheel." *Review of Educational Research* 78: 552–88.

Thompson, Chastity Q. 2006. "Recruitment, Retention, and Mentoring Faculty of Color: The Chronicle Continues." *New Directions for Higher Education* 143: 47–54.

Victorino, Christine A., Karen Nylund-Gibson, and Sharon Conley. 2013. "Campus Racial Climate: A Litmus Test for Faculty Satisfaction at Four-Year Colleges and Universities." *Journal of Higher Education* 84 (6): 769–805.

Ward, LaWanda. 2008. "Female Faculty in Male-Dominated Fields: Law, Medicine, and Engineering." *Faculty at the Margins*, special issue, 143: 63–72.

Wennerås, Christine, and Agnes Wold. 1997. "Nepotism and Sexism in Peer-Review." *Nature* 387: 341–43.

Winkler, Julie A. 2000. "Faculty Reappointment, Tenure and Promotion: Barriers for Women." *Professional Geographer* 52 (4): 737–50.

Index

About the Author

Tammy Stone received her PhD from the Department of Anthropology, Arizona State University, where she specialized in the archaeology of the American Southwest. She has been at the University of Colorado Denver since 1992 and is the recipient of a number of awards in teaching, research, and service/leadership. Her interest in higher education administration grew as she took on an increasing number of leadership positions. In addition to archaeology, she has published on teaching, mentoring, the development of interdisciplinary programs, and leading departments that have been placed in receivership. In 2011 she coauthored *Leading from the Middle: A Case-Study Approach to Academic Leadership for Associate Deans*, published by Rowman & Littlefield.

Lightning Source UK Ltd.
Milton Keynes UK
UKHW01f2016140818
327229UK00001B/40/P